*Ja Jonelfm.*

# Gospel for the Outsider

*The Gospel in Luke & Acts*

— PATRICK WHITWORTH —

*with every blessing*

**Sacristy**
Press

**Sacristy Press**
PO Box 612, Durham, DH1 9HT

www.sacristy.co.uk

First published in 2014 by Sacristy Press, Durham

Copyright © Patrick Whitworth 2014
The moral rights of the author have been asserted

Sacristy Limited, registered in England & Wales, number 7565667

**British Library Cataloguing-in-Publication Data**
A catalogue record for the book is available from the British Library

ISBN 978-1-908381-24-8

*To Luke Wheeler-Mezei,*
*a courageous and gracious boy.*

# Foreword

The twenty-first century is proving to be an interesting time. Likened by one commentator to being cast adrift in tossing seas on a raft with no map, it seems as if many of the assumptions which have sustained us over the centuries are beginning to lose their reassuring solidity. In particular, the founding modern myth of progress is being undermined by whispering suggestions that economically, geopolitically, and even medically we may be heading not further into the ever increasing prosperity to which we have become accustomed, but unnervingly in the opposite direction. As our anxiety grows, the question emerges with growing frequency: how best to live in this uncertain place?

This book does not address the question of the tossing seas. It does something rather more important: it helps us to find an anchor with which to withstand them—the anchor offered by Luke, the third gospel writer and the one who took a particular interest in those who found themselves excluded from the comfort of the prevailing framework of society. It is generally recognised that each of the four gospel writers has his own particular perspective. For Mark, it's the call to discipleship—the invitation to follow Jesus and shape your life according to his teaching. For Matthew, it's the way in which the coming of Jesus fulfils all that has gone before. For young John, it's relationships, and the formation of a new kind of community. And, for Luke, it's ministry, and in particular ministry to the outsider—the outsider who, as Patrick so clearly and beautifully demonstrates, becomes the insider through his or her encounter with Jesus.

The differences between these complementary emphases are found in the opening chapters of the four gospels. Mark bursts into print with the prophetic announcement of the coming of a Saviour. John offers a reflection on the relationship between Father, Son, and Spirit which underpins the whole of reality. Matthew concentrates on getting the genealogy right. And Luke—Luke talks about unexpected visits from angels to unimportant people, starting not with kings and seers like Matthew, but in the fields with a bunch of ordinary working shepherds. Into his unfolding narrative creep disabled men, fallen women, foreign soldiers, and stories about street-muggings and spendthrift children. Mark may challenge you, Matthew reassure you, and John inspire you, but it is among the real people of Luke's gospel that you will find yourself. And that, I suggest, is the task of our times—to find ourselves, to discover who we are and how it is that we can play our part in shaping a new world.

Driving north on the M1 the other day I found myself behind a lorry with a message. In big letters on the back it proclaimed: "If you can't be yourself, you will make a lousy someone else." I think that is Luke's message too. Don't worry about how the world defines you, or try to fit in with its failing assumptions about what it means to live successfully. Find out who you are, and be that person. That, I think, is the message Luke brings to us in his gospel; for it is only as we encounter Jesus that our lives begin to make sense. And it is the message that Patrick unfolds in this readable, compelling invitation to walk into the story and find yourself, whoever you may be, within its pages.

**Alison Morgan**
*ReSource, Wells*
*October 2014*

# Preface

I hope this book will be the first of a series on each of the four Gospels highlighting the "USPs" (unique selling points) of each Gospel. We know that three—Matthew, Mark, and Luke—are similar. We call them synoptic Gospels, as they share much common material. John's Gospel, we know, is quite distinct, called by one early Church Father, Clement of Alexandria, "the spiritual gospel". But in this short study-volume we are looking at Luke and the presentation of the gospel within Luke/Acts, Luke's great two-volume work. What we are looking for is the gospel within the Gospel—the good news within the Gospel Luke wrote, which we simply call Luke's Gospel. The good news, of course, centres on Jesus himself: his forgiveness and mercy to all people, and the presence of the Kingdom. This is clearly shown in the Gospel and then extended through the Acts; firstly in Jerusalem, then on the missionary journeys of the Apostle Paul. Luke accompanied Paul for the last two journeys, at least in part, and was with him in Rome at the end.

The gospel within the Gospel for Luke was that this good news was for the outsider in Jewish society, and indeed for any outsider in any society where the sleek, the successful, and the slick are often preferred to the loser, the lonely, and the lowly. Luke is the only Gentile writer in the scriptures, and his Gospel has a marked bias to the outsider, the one who can be neglected, discarded, or simply overlooked. Luke gives us three stories which marvellously illustrate this gospel within a Gospel and are unique to him: the ever-waiting Father, waiting for the return of the Prodigal son; the ever-vigilant Jesus, looking up to call down Zacchaeus from a sycamore tree; and the ever-merciful Saviour Christ responding to the penitent thief next to him on the cross. These together demonstrate the heart of the Gospel, and the heart of Jesus for the outcast or the outsider. In this book I hope to show that this compassion for the outsider is clear from several angles. I hope too that it will direct our mission to those who, in whatever shape or form, are outsiders today in our communities. That might be a despised banker, a paedophile, or even a jihadist. What we can be sure of is that Jesus' mercy goes way beyond our own, in shocking grace, looking for just a flicker of repentance and a sliver of belief. This Gospel is a gospel for the outsider. In our day it has been iconically illustrated by Pope Francis embracing Vinicio Riva, a deeply disfigured man with neurofibromatosis and shunned by many.

I hope that, with the help of the study guide at the end, there will be an opportunity for groups to study the Gospel from this point of view. More importantly, I hope it will help us to discern the outsiders in our own communities and go to them with the love of Christ and the hope of the gospel—a gospel for outsiders.

Finally, I must thank all those who have helped me with the production of this book: All Saints Weston, who a few years ago patiently listened to a formative series of teaching on Luke's Gospel with the same title as this book. I also thank Ann Banner and Gay Ridley in the processing of the book as it came together, and with helping with the bibliography; Alison Morgan for kindly writing the Foreword; and Sacristy Press for their support during the production. Finally, I would like to thank my family and especially Olivia, my wife, for encouraging me and putting up with all too frequent absences when I might have been doing something useful like gardening instead!

**Patrick Whitworth**
*4 October 2014*

# Contents

# Introduction

This is not so much a commentary as a considered look at the writings of Luke from one particular point of view; the point of view which is, in fact, dominant in Luke's writings. He wrote with the *outsider* sharply in focus, and this is what I hope to show as we look at his two great books in the New Testament: his gospel, and the Acts of the Apostles.

Before we launch into demonstrating this from his writings, a word is needed about his authorship, his own background, his sources, and the construction of his two great works. That Luke is the author of both Acts and the gospel which bears his name is easily demonstrated. The author of the third gospel is also the author of Acts. He tells us as much in the opening sentence of Acts: "in my former book, Theophilus, I wrote about all that Jesus began to do and to teach" (Acts 1:1). The Author of Acts is a companion of Paul. There are several occasions when the author of Acts makes it clear that he was *with* Paul. These so-called *we sections* are found in the following passages: Acts 16:10ff, when Luke accompanies Paul to Troas before the call to go over to Macedonia to preach the gospel; Acts 16:16ff when a female fortune teller pursued Paul, Luke, and others through the Philippi; Acts 20:5ff and 21:1ff, when Luke accompanies Paul on his journey to James, the leader of the church in Jerusalem; and finally from Acts 27:1ff when Luke accompanies Paul on his voyage to Rome (Acts 28:16). Furthermore, Paul himself makes clear his close association with Luke: on three occasions Paul refers to his beloved companion and physician Luke as being with him during his imprisonment in Rome (see Colossians 4:14, Philemon 24, and 2 Timothy 4:9).

Luke was, therefore, Paul's faithful companion; a physician who travelled extensively with Paul from his second missionary journey onwards, visiting Philippi, Ephesus, and Troas, and maybe other places besides, before returning with Paul to Jerusalem and then travelling with him on his final voyage to Rome. It is as well to remember this and the deep influence that Paul would have had on him when we come to consider the way in which Luke wrote his gospel. It has been said that if the Petrine Gospel (i.e. the gospel and narrative handed down by Peter to John Mark in Rome in *c.* AD 64) is to be found in Mark's Gospel, then the Pauline Gospel is to be found beautifully crafted into Luke's work. In other words, what Peter was to Mark, Paul was to Luke. But Luke has his own take, his own slant and insight, which makes his work very much unique, as we shall see.

What the biblical evidence suggests, the early Fathers confirm. Irenaeus (*c.* AD 180) names the companion of Paul as the author of Luke and Acts; Clement of Alexandria (*c.* AD 190–242) quotes from the gospel frequently, and ascribes it to Luke. Likewise Tertullian, in his anti-Marcionite writings, frequently refers to the third Gospel which he ascribes to Luke. There was no doubt in the early years of the Church's life, and its earliest compilation of the scriptures in the Muratorian Canon made in Rome between AD 170–200, that Luke was uniformly regarded as the author of the third gospel.[1]

The gospel writers were quite different from each other, providing contrasting accounts of the life, ministry, and passion of Jesus. These four witnesses have been characterised as the Rebel (Mark), the Rabbi (Matthew), the Chronicler (Luke), and the Mystic (John). Although three of them shared common material, they each crafted a distinct account of the life of Jesus of Nazareth.[2]

In some ways, however, Luke is the gospel writer least familiar to the Apostolic community. He was the only Gospel writer who was one stage removed from the original Apostolic community. By contrast, Matthew and John were themselves Apostles, and John Mark, it appears, was on the fringe of that group, and was present at events during the Passion. He was known to have been present at the arrest of Jesus in the garden of Gethsemane; he was thought to have been the man who fled naked when detained by the Temple guard (Mark 14:51–52). The cousin of Barnabas, he accompanied Paul on his first missionary journey but soon turned back (Acts 13:13) at Pisidian Antioch. Paul refused to take him on his second missionary, causing a split with Barnabas who stood by his cousin John Mark (Acts 15:36ff). But the relationship with Paul was restored, and we find Mark assisting Paul in Rome (2 Timothy 4:11b) and becoming the interpreter of Peter, writing a Gospel based on his memories in Rome in *c.* AD 64 (1 Peter 5:13). Matthew was himself one of the Apostles. Called by Jesus from tax gathering (Matthew 9:9), he found a vocation as a systematic teacher of the faith to the Jewish community. He wrote the most Jewish gospel, and one that is *the* most comprehensive guide to discipleship. Finally, John was one of the inner-circle of Apostles along with Peter and his brother James. Almost certainly the last of the Gospel writers in *c.* AD 90 in Ephesus, John most probably knew of the existence of the other Gospels and wrote what Clement called a "spiritual gospel"; highly crafted, extremely selective in its material, and written for both the Gentile community in Asia and the Hellenised Jews in the dispersion.[3]

Luke's claim to apostolicity, however, rested on his close association with Paul. Much of the clue to Luke's identity lies in his name. His name may well have been an abbreviation of a longer Greek name: 'Lucanus', 'Lucilus', or 'Lucianius' were all relatively common. Although some Jews had Greek names such as Philip, Luke was almost certainly Greek himself, and therefore a Gentile. His name is listed among the non-Jewish or Gentile list of Pauline associates in Colossians 4:12ff. As a Gentile, Luke was the only non-Jewish author in the New Testament. Thus it is not surprising that the focus of his Gospel is the Gentile world, reflecting both his own ethnicity and his close association with Paul, the Apostle to the Gentiles. Luke then, by birth, background, and through mission, was *the* Gospel writer for the outsider: the message he had was that Jesus was the Saviour of all nations. Not only is it the gospel for the outsider, more fundamentally, Luke supremely portrayed Jesus as the Saviour of the world.

Luke was most probably a Gentile from either Antioch or Tarsus. Of the two towns, it may be more likely that he came from Antioch, one of the great cities of the Roman Empire and where the early Church flourished: it was at Antioch that the followers of the Way were first called Christians (Acts 11:20ff). It was a substantial Church with a large number of Gentile Christians. Barnabas, who was sent there from Jerusalem to help the development of the church, quickly saw the need for Paul's teaching and skills in discipleship. He brought him from Tarsus, and for a year they both taught and encouraged the Church. Is it far-fetched to think that Luke was part of the congregation there; a young doctor with literary and writing skills and a missionary heart? Although he did not accompany Paul on his first missionary journey to Cyprus and the interior of Asia, he was more than ready to go with Paul on his second missionary journey to Europe and accompanied him thereafter. At some point during or following these travels, Luke must have had the idea of writing a gospel for the Gentile world, as well as an account of the beginning of the Church. He was perhaps encouraged by Paul, which reflected his background, experience, and convictions. An unusually skilled writer and chronicler, Luke's contribution to the New Testament was to be larger than any other, and he has given us arguably the most attractive, compassionate, and inclusive picture of Jesus and his Kingdom of all the New Testament authors.

Traditionally the most favoured date for the writing of the third gospel has been around AD 65. The fact that that the Gospel appears to be written before the destruction of the Temple and Jerusalem, and that there is no mention of Paul's execution in Rome, leads many scholars to suppose that both volumes were written before the outbreak of Nero's persecution of the Church following the great fire of Rome in AD 64. If Luke joined Paul's second missionary journey which began in AD 49, and stayed with him until his eventual arrival in Rome AD 60, then there was ample time to begin and complete his two-volume work. Indeed there were long periods of time in which Luke might have undertaken further research; for instance during Paul's long imprisonment in Caesarea from AD 57–59. There was time then to meet key witnesses of the ministry and life of Jesus, to assemble material, and begin the careful business of writing. Luke's time in Rome would also have put him in touch with the writings of John Mark and the memories of Peter, both of whom lived there (1 Peter 5:13). Furthermore, whilst assembling this material and being part of the missionary journeys, there was time and opportunity to reflect on the teaching that Paul gave the Church both in his letters and in person.

As he tells us himself, Luke's writing had a clear aim: "to write an orderly account" for the most excellent Theophilus. He devoted both the Gospel and Acts to the "most excellent Theophilus" (Luke 1:3 and Acts 1:1). 'Theophilus' means 'lover of God' and, in the ancient world, this was probably a polite form of address to a person of higher social standing, who in this case was most likely a Gentile believer. This person was almost certainly a real individual rather than a symbolic figure or literary device, and was quite possibly a Gentile Roman official for whom both volumes of Luke's work were a serious apologetic, making clear both the certainty and veracity of the message and the goodness of its effect. Luke makes no claim for himself as an original eyewitness to the life of Jesus (Luke 1:2), but rather he says that he has carefully investigated the whole story and message of Jesus and has now produced an "orderly account" (1:3). What follows is a very well written and sophisticated narrative of the life and ministry of Jesus in two volumes: firstly what Jesus himself did, and then what he continued to do through the activity of the Spirit in the Church (Acts 1:1).

Luke's investigations were extensive and comprehensive. Scholars are convinced that he had at least three main sources for his gospel.[4] Firstly, he already had a copy of Mark's gospel and he included a large proportion of Mark's material in his own gospel. It is thought that about 40 per cent of Luke's Gospel was taken directly from Mark.[5] Matthew includes an even higher proportion of Mark in his gospel. In addition, Luke relied on two other main sources, which theologians label Q and L. Q simply stands for 'quelle', the German word for 'source', and this is thought to be an eclectic collection of Jesus' sayings. Matthew also uses this collection, and it has traditionally been considered a principal source for the text of the Lord's Prayer. However, the absence of knowledge among the early Church Fathers of the existence of such an independent source is one of the puzzles of biblical scholarship.[6] Another source, which is unique to Luke, is simply called L. Material unique to Luke was thought to be taken from this source. Birth narratives such as the Annunciation, the *Magnificat,* and those concerned with the birth of John the Baptist might have been taken from L. Scholars have concluded that 45 per cent of Luke is taken from Mark; 23 per cent from the common source Q, which both Matthew and Luke used; and that a further 35 per cent of Luke was taken from L.[7] But this may be all too tidy and it could be argued that the part of the gospel unique to Luke was taken from a number of different sources, not least Mary herself, who may have given Luke his infancy narratives, as suggested by the personal nature of these reflections and reminiscences (see Luke 2:17). Whatever the correct analysis of sources, Luke, like Matthew, has given us a very well researched gospel. The material was painstakingly

and diligently collected, but more than that it was then compiled in both
an elegant orderly way whilst maintaining a clear theological perspective.

Different types of what came to be called biblical criticism concentrated
on different aspects of gospel–writing. *Form criticism* focused on the way
sources were handed down in textual forms, although some well-known
critics sought to shave anything they deemed 'myth' from such accounts.
Any material which contained examples of the supernatural power of
Jesus was discarded by these rationalising form critics as problematic
ecclesiastical fiction. Thus, a tool which might simply have been used to
trace source material via identification of different textual forms came
to be used as means of stripping away material that the critics regarded
as Church fabrications. Such critics moved from being merely textual
critics to being judges and arbiters of scriptural veracity. Much of this was
done with the ostensibly laudable aim of reaching the real historical Jesus,
shorn of all accretions. In actuality, such criticism reveals more about a
world-view in which supernatural intervention is deemed outlandish than
it does about the scriptural text it supposedly illuminates.

A more sensitive and fruitful critical model can be found in what
is termed 'redaction criticism'. This involves looking at the author, say
of one of the Gospels, as an editor or redactor; i.e. one who assembled
and arranged material in a particular way. Rooted in 1940s German
theology, the main modern advocates of redaction criticism were Hans
Conzelmann and Gunther Bornkamm, both of whom were influenced
by Rudolf Bultmann.[8] Conzelmann, who made a special study of Luke,
engaged in the debate about whether Luke was more historian than
theologian. It is no doubt fair to say that Luke was a careful historian
seeking to present his material in a genuine historical narrative; hence
his noting to Theophilus that he was writing him an "orderly account"
(1:3). However, to say that Luke was *only* an historian would be to sell
his reflection and theological presentation short. We must imagine Luke
as having assembled his aforementioned sources and seeking to shape
them into a gospel. We must seek to establish his influences and ask
how they shaped his editorial processes. Or to put it a different way, we
need to ask what theological drivers motivated him. As an editor, he was
seeking to give a faithful, accurate, and elegant account of Jesus' ministry.
Nonetheless, whatever made him include some things and exclude others

was not merely an historical imperative but a deeper theological one; a desire to present Jesus and the salvation he brought in a particular light. The main theological perspective which motivated the way Luke assembled and presented his material was that Jesus was the Saviour of *all* people. This fundamental premise is spelt out in a particularly inclusive way throughout the course of Luke's text. Jesus was the saviour of women, of the weak and lowly, of the poor, of the outsider (much of this is present in the *Magnificat*). In short, the Saviour had come to seek and save the marginalised and the lost. These considerations were shaped no doubt by Luke's own Gentile origins, by having been around Paul during his preaching through Europe, and by his time in Rome. For Luke, Jesus was the supreme crosser of divides! And what is especially telling is that, of the twenty-three parables that Jesus tells in Luke's Gospel, only five are found elsewhere. In other words, eighteen are unique to Luke.[9] It is worth reminding ourselves that without Luke there would be no parable of the Prodigal Son or Good Samaritan, nor the Great Supper or the Friend at midnight, nor of the Pharisee and the Publican. So a good question to ask is: what do these parables singularly convey? What was it that drove Luke to include them uniquely in his gospel? What were the theological reasons that made him as editor or redactor present them? And what understanding of Jesus do we have from their inclusion, which otherwise we might not have had? Hopefully, by the end of the book, we will be better able to answer these questions.

In summary then, Luke writes a gospel with several distinct emphases. He presents a gospel for the Gentile world; replacing Jewish terms with better known Greek ones (for instance replacing 'Rabbi' with 'Master'). He esteems the importance of women and the significance of domestic life. He demonstrates the vitality and efficacy of prayer. He shows the working of the Holy Spirit with a freshness and immediacy unknown in the other gospel writers, especially in the infancy narratives. He shows that it is a universal gospel with a Saviour who is the Saviour of the World; finding a uniform response of praise to his salvation work. All this is woven into an elegant and well-ordered narrative: starting with his unique infancy narratives, the Gospel moves through the ministry of John the Baptist (3:1–4:13), Jesus' ministry in Galilee (4:14–9:50), his journey to Jerusalem (9:51–19:27), his ministry in Jerusalem (19:28–21:38), and lastly his Passion, crucifixion, and resurrection (21:1–24:53). This diligent record is galvanised by Luke's consistently emphatic conviction that the ministry of Jesus, from infancy to resurrection, was directed to the outsider. It is this theme, I hope, that we shall follow, reveal, and celebrate in the chapters ahead.

C H A P T E R   1

# Outsiders at the Birth of Christ

To say that Luke was the only gospel writer who focused on outsiders at the nativity would be an overstatement. Matthew (albeit using different sources) also demonstrates the significance of outsiders: the visit of the Magi and the genealogy of Jesus both bear witness to this. The Magi are endlessly fascinating in their origin, belonging either to the Persian priestly caste or to the ruling class of some distinctive religion, or a people with strong astrological knowledge.[10] They were certainly outsiders, following a star for many hundreds of miles until they found and worshipped the infant king with their presents of gold, frankincense, and myrrh.

Matthew also hinted at the destiny of the Messiah as Saviour of the world by including outsiders in his intriguing genealogy of Jesus (Matthew 1:1–17). Placed at the outset of the Gospel and divided into three blocks of fourteen generations each from Abraham to David, David to the Exile, and from the Exile to Jesus (Matthew 1:17), Matthew mentions five women, some of colourful reputation, in an otherwise all male list of Jewish ancestry. They are Tamar, Rahab, Ruth, Bathsheba (mentioned interestingly as the wife of Uriah the Hittite), and Mary. Ruth and Mary were devout; Ruth was a non-Israelite. Tamar procured a child and heir by crafty and illicit intercourse with Judah, her father-in-law, in an extraordinary interlude to the Joseph story (see Genesis 38). Rahab was the prostitute who recognised the presence of God with the invading armies of Israel in the conquest of her native land, Canaan, as a result hiding their spies (Joshua 2:8). Bathsheba needs little introduction. She was the beauty whom David fell for when he was looking out of a window rather than going out to war (2 Samuel 11:1–3). From these women Jesus was descended. Several were not Jews, nor were they especially pious, but neither, for that matter, were many of the men.

If in Matthew's Gospel there is a clear sense of the Christ being born *from* mixed racial ancestry and *for* the nations, in Luke's account the idea of Jesus' birth being for the outsider is equally clear. In Luke we do not have Magi from the East, but poor shepherds. We do not have a genealogy placed before the birth of Jesus like a herald's announcement before the birth of a prince, but we have a genealogy of 77 generations tracing Jesus neatly back to God (Luke 3:23–37). This genealogy is placed not before the birth of Jesus, confirming his human ancestry as in Matthew, but before the outset of his ministry. Again in Luke we have a telling comparison between the response of the *insider* Zechariah to the angelic news of a longed for child, and a much more faith-filled response by the *outsider* Mary to the news that she will have a child outside her union with Joseph. We have an additional comparison between the domestic arrangements of a family caught in Imperial policy, and the fate of the Empire itself. And, lastly, in Luke we have the spontaneous, Spirit-inspired utterances of praise, which place the *outsider* at the centre of God's plan of salvation. Such emphases appear at the beginning of Luke's Gospel and continue to the very end.

## Zechariah and Mary

The initial contrast in Luke's Gospel is both between John the Baptist and Jesus, and between Zechariah and Mary. John the Baptist is the last of the Jewish prophets; Jesus is the Saviour of the world. The former was to bring Israel to repentance, preaching a baptism of repentance for the forgiveness of sins, while Jesus would make possible that forgiveness through his death and give the Holy Spirit to the nations (Acts 3:16b). Likewise in Acts, salvation would be made known to outsiders: to the Jews from the Diaspora who were visiting in Jerusalem at Pentecost (Acts 2:5), then to the Samaritans, and lastly to the Gentiles as represented by Cornelius' household (Acts 10:47). Paul would then take the Gospel to communities throughout the Empire. But John was the essential precursor to Jesus, preparing the nation for him spiritually, until Jesus opened the Kingdom to all peoples. Likewise Mary was the willing "vessel" for the Messiah whereas Zechariah was the astonished and unbelieving father of the final prophet of Israel. We can compare the two as *insider* and *outsider*.

Zechariah, if we can put it like this, was the *insider*. He was a priest, one of about 18,000 in Israel. The Jewish priesthood was divided into twenty-four courses, each composed of four to nine families. And, apart from the great festivals, they performed their duties for only two separate weeks a year.[11] Zechariah's family belonged to the priestly division of Abijah, eighth in the list of the divisions (see 1 Chronicles 24:10). He was married to Elizabeth, the name shared by Aaron's wife (Exodus 6:23) meaning "God is my fortune". Elizabeth was also of priestly stock, being descended from Aaron himself. They were both of impeccable Levite pedigree but they were unable to have children.

One day during his priestly service in the Temple, Zechariah was chosen by lot to burn incense in the sanctuary. This was a once-in-a-lifetime opportunity to enter the Sanctuary (not the Holiest of Holies which only the High Priest could enter once a year on the day of Atonement) and burn incense; a symbol of prayer at the time of the evening sacrifice. While the Priest burnt incense on the burning coals the people outside the holy place would pray, "May the merciful God enter the holy place and accept the offering of his people".[12] Perhaps the words of Psalm 141:2 were recalled, "Let my prayer be counted as incense before you, and the lifting up of my hands as an evening sacrifice". It was while this most precious moment in Zacariah's life occurred that the Angel Gabriel appeared with his message. Elizabeth, he said, was to have a child, and he would be special; John will be:

> A joy and delight to you, and many will rejoice because of
> his birth, for he will be great in the sight of the Lord . . .
> He will be filled with the Holy Spirit even from birth . . .
> Many of the people of Israel he will bring back to the Lord
> their God.
>
> *Luke 1:14–16*

But Zechariah's response was not all that it might have been: "How can I be sure of this? I am an old man and my wife is well on in years" (Luke 1:18). For such an uncertain and unbelieving response, not dissimilar to Sarah's in Genesis 18:12, Zechariah was punished by being made dumb. The people, no doubt wondering what had happened to Zechariah on his big day, rightly concluded that God had appeared to him in some way (Luke 1:22). He returned home and Elizabeth became pregnant (1:24). But, in contrast, the young teenage girl, the comparative outsider in Israel compared with Zechariah and confronted by an even more extraordinary prospect through the same angel, responded quite differently.

Mary was betrothed to be married to Joseph, a descendant of David. Engagement could be embarked on then by a girl as young as twelve. It probably lasted up to a year and was arranged by the families concerned.[13] Betrothal was considered as binding as marriage, the couple being regarded as virtually legally married. It was not normal for sexual intercourse to take place during this period. It was during such a time that the Angel Gabriel appeared to Mary, announcing that she would have a child. At the news she was described as "greatly troubled" (1:29). Despite this she responds thoughtfully and profoundly to the word spoken to her by Gabriel, as Ratzinger points out:

> Mary appears as a fearless woman, one who remains composed even in the presence of something utterly unprecedented. At the same time she stands before us as a woman of great interiority, who holds heart and mind in harmony and seeks to understand the context, the overall significance of God's message.[14]

The fact that she would be pregnant at some point in the future could not have been too surprising since she was already betrothed. So her question, "How will this be now since I am only a virgin?" (1:34) arises not so much from how she will become pregnant—for that would be her normal expectation after marriage—so much as how *this child* prophesied by the Angel who will "be great and will be called the Son of the Most High" (1:32a) will be conceived. The question thus shows remarkable presence of mind and perception on Mary's part, in that she must have not only have understood Gabriel's message of her giving birth to the Messiah, but at the same time also must have wondered how that could this come about outside of her marriage to Joseph. She was told: "The Holy Spirit will come upon you, and the power of the Most High will overshadow you. So the Holy one to be born will be called the Son of God" (1:35). That Elizabeth, her cousin or relative, was already six months pregnant despite having given up hope provided further proof.

What follows is a distinctly different response to that of Zechariah: compared to his "how can I be sure of this" (1:18a), Mary replies staggeringly, "I am the Lord's servant. May it be to me as you have said" (1:38). Mary the teenage bride, a girl seemingly plucked from obscurity with no Jewish roots mentioned in the scriptures apart from her family ties to Elizabeth, accedes calmly to the news that she will bear the Messiah, the Son of God.[15] An Israelite yet still a comparative outsider, a teenage mother-to-be now lies at the centre of God's will. It is to be a theme throughout Luke's Gospel and the book of Acts: the weak, the rejected, the isolated, the despised, the foreigner, all take centre stage in God's plan. Their comparative worldviews are expressed in their prophetic songs, which accompany the meeting of Mary and Elizabeth and the birth of John the Baptist.

## The Songs of Mary and Zechariah

Zechariah's ministry at the heart of the religious establishment of Israel was clearly very much one of an insider, especially since he and Elizabeth were also personally "righteous before God, living blamelessly according to all the commandments and regulations of the Lord" (1:6). By contrast, Mary's faith and insight are all the more remarkable. Mary, as a low born bride-to-be of a carpenter (1:48) was more of an outsider. It is possible to trace their respective religious and social positions reflected in their two great prophetic songs recorded by Luke. It is clear that both songs, which we know as Mary's Song (the *Magnificat*) and Zechariah's Song, arose not only from the circumstances that gave them birth, but also from the promises given to each by the angel Gabriel about their respective sons.

Mary's song was given voice by her meeting with Elizabeth, six months ahead of her in her pregnancy (1:36b). At the meeting of the two expectant mothers, the neonate John the Baptist leapt in his mother's womb for joy (1:44). The two children were to be inextricably linked in their lives and ministry: both were to suffer execution as a result of their calling; both were to bring joy and hope to their followers. And Elizabeth recognised prophetically the faith of Mary: "blessed is she who believed that there would be a fulfilment of what was spoken to her by the Lord that the child within Mary was promised by God" (1:45). Mary's response to this insight is her song of praise. In Luke, praise is the spontaneous result of God's working. The theme of the song is praise to God for his essential nature: he is the one who raises the humble and lowly and who humbles the proud and powerful. This is what he has done for Mary, and this is what he will always do. Conversely, he is also the one who "scatters the proud" (1:51), who "brings down the powerful" (1:52) "who sends the rich away empty" (1:53). This is the way God works in the salvation He brings; not only to Mary herself but also to Israel as a whole, to whom God is now fulfilling his promise made generations ago to Abraham (1:55). In many ways it is the song of an outsider.

Zechariah's song comes in a very different context. John has now been born, and he is about to be circumcised on the eighth day, according to the Law. Zechariah, still dumb, confirms by writing on a slate that his son is to be called John, as Elizabeth has already indicated at the assembled gathering. At that moment Zechariah regains his speech and his song pours forth, directed by the Spirit in a prophetic celebration. Zechariah knows that the saviour or horn of salvation is coming (1:69); he knows that the promise sworn to Abraham is about to be fulfilled in the birth of the Messiah (1:72-73) and that his son John is to be the forerunner or the prophet of the Most High (1:76). If Mary's song exalts a king and a kingdom to come which loves humility and hates human pride, in keeping with the promises made to David, Zechariah's song not only rejoices in that but also shows the need for a prophet to accompany the King in his mission. Coming from within the Aaronic priesthood, John was to be another great outsider (living ascetically in the desert) in the gospel, summoning people to repentance in preparation for receiving the Messiah. After all, Luke tells us that "he was in the wilderness until the day he appeared publicly to Israel" (1:80b).

## The Emperor and a New Empire

Much of Jesus' early life was spent under the rule of Octavian, given the title Augustus in 27 BC. It was Octavian—the posthumously adopted heir of the Julius Caesar who had been assassinated on the Ides of March in 44 BC—who brought both great expansion and peace (*Pax Romana*) to the Roman Empire. Initially, with Mark Anthony and Lepidus, Octavian formed the Second Triumvirate and took on the killers of Julius Caesar, Brutus and Cassius, defeating them at the Battle of Philippi in 42 BC and forming the Second Triumvirate. But Mark Anthony's separation from Octavian's sister for the fascinating charms of Cleopatra, and his formation of an alliance with Egypt against Rome, precipitated war with Octavian. Anthony was defeated at the sea battle of Actium and then again at Alexandria itself, where he and Cleopatra committed suicide, as recalled so powerfully and poignantly by Shakespeare. Three years later, Octavian was titled Augustus. From 27 BC to AD 27 he ruled supreme in an ever-expanding empire.[16]

In the eastern part of the Empire, Augustus' power was ever increasing. Egypt, with its vast corn reserves from the Nile Delta, became part of the Empire from 30 BC onwards and would remain so until the Islamic Rashidun Caliphate swept through North Africa in the seventh century. Ships with grain from Alexandria would feed the burgeoning population of Rome. By the time Luke wrote his gospel the population of Rome, standing at a million, was kept in bread by the grain fields of North Africa and in circuses by Emperors keen for the support of the populace. In Judea the client king of Rome, Herod the Great, would ingratiate himself with the Jewish population by re-building the Temple. It continued to be built throughout Jesus's life, so massive was its construction. Herod died in 4 BC, soon after the birth of Jesus. Judea was then incorporated into the

Roman province of Syria with its capital at the great city of Antioch, which became important to Luke's narrative in the Acts of the Apostles. The church at Antioch, so large and diverse, would become the springboard for missions to the whole of the Western Roman Empire (see Acts 13:13ff).

In 4 BC a virtually unknown couple in a far-flung corner of the Empire, with an unusual domestic story of family life, responded to an edict from the newly established Governor of Syria, Quirinius (with powers over Judea since the death of Herod the Great), to register in their hometown. Joseph and the heavily pregnant Mary made their way from Nazareth to Bethlehem. The regular census of his subjects was a mark of the new Imperial policy of Augustus. Although there is no other record of a universal census being taken in the Empire in 4 BC, there were several separate censuses in Roman provinces, and with the increasing power of the Province of Syria in the affairs of Judea, there was good reason for a census at this point.[17] Exactly why Joseph felt the need to go to Bethlehem is not clear: he may have been born there, had family, or even owned some property there. The only reason Luke gives us is that Joseph "belonged to the house and line of David" (Luke 2:4). At any rate, Joseph believed that it was in Bethlehem that he would be expected to register.

With our outsider/insider theme for this study of Luke's Gospel and the book of Acts, there emerges a further deeper vein of thought to explore. Luke was no stranger himself to Imperial power. After all, before he wrote this gospel, if our conjectures in the Introduction are right, the gospel was researched and written either soon after Luke's journey to Rome with Paul (see Acts 27) or in part before. We know that Luke was there with Paul in Rome (AD 56?) as Paul records in his prison letter to Timothy, "Only Luke is with me" (2 Timothy 4:11). So Luke knew, at first hand, the workings of Imperial power whether in Philippi, Ephesus, or Rome. He knew its flavour, its power, its brutality, and its destiny. But he also knew that with the advent of Jesus, a greater Kingdom had been born into the world, and that a greater King had come (Luke 23:3). Jesus would talk about this kingdom continuously in his parables, many of which Luke includes in his gospel. So it is quite likely that in the back of his mind, indeed maybe in the very forefront of his thoughts, there was the idea that Joseph and Mary, summoned by Imperial edict to Bethlehem, were to give birth to a king and kingdom which would outlive, outshine and outdo all other kingdoms, including this Empire based in Rome with its Emperor claiming divine status. The prophecies of Daniel would be fulfilled (Daniel 7:9ff), and:

> one like the Son of Man approached the Ancient of Days and was led into his presence. He was given authority, glory and sovereign power; all peoples, nations and men of every language worshipped him. His dominion is an everlasting dominion that will not pass away, and his kingdom is one that will never be destroyed.
>
> *Daniel 7:13-14*

This child, born in an obscure part of the Empire as a result of an Imperial edict, was not only the inheritor of all the promises of David, but the long awaited Messiah: the anointed King. The one who appeared as an inconsequential carpenter from unprepossessing town—an outsider – would in fact establish a kingdom surpassing and outliving every other. But it did not look that way, certainly not at first.


## A Stable and Shepherds

An unusual collection of people went to an equally unusual maternity unit to see a baby heralded either by a star or by a choir of angels on the hillside. It is Luke who plainly tells us, "While they were there [Bethlehem], the time came for the baby to be born, and she wrapped him in cloths and placed him in a manger, because there was no room in the inn" (2:6–7). Matthew tells us of the coming of the Magi immediately after informing us of the birth of Jesus (Matthew 2:1–12), although it may have been some months or even years till the arrival of the Wise Men. What is clear from Luke was that there was no room in the guest room or inn ('*kataluma*', literally meaning 'lodging'). The point that Luke is recording is that there was no place to be found in normal human habitation, so Jesus was born in a place commonly used for sheltering animals. A place where there was a manger. Kenneth Bailey makes the point that Jesus was probably born in a room or space commonly used for animals in a home where animals were frequently kept below the living accommodation of a family.[18] And there being no crib or cot, Jesus was placed in the only available place for a baby, a manger. Another tradition dating back to the second century was that Jesus was born in a hillside cave, like the one to be found today in the Basilica in Bethlehem, erected by Constantine in the early fourth century and which is now the Church of the Nativity.

Whether in a cave or stall, it was there that the Shepherds came in response to the message of the angels. These first visitors to the infant Christ and holy family found what they had been told by the angels,

> Today in the town of David a Saviour has been born to you: he is the Christ the Lord. This shall be a sign to you [so unique was this nativity scene]. You will find a baby wrapped in cloths and lying in a manger . . . And so it was just as they had been told.
>
> *Luke 2:11–12, 16–17*

The shepherds were, on the one hand, symbolic of Jesus's ministry, and, on the other hand, indicative of the humility of Jesus' birth. Shepherding was considered by the Jews to be a dirty profession and its members were therefore part of religiously suspect group. For them to be the first visitors to the Nativity was a further sign that Jesus' coming was for the poor, the despised, and the lowly, embodied by this ordinary bunch of shepherds. But the shepherds also foreshadowed the ministry of Jesus, who described himself as the Good Shepherd (John 10: 11a), the successor to David, the shepherd psalmist in whose city he was born. Jesus had come to shepherd his people, the prophet Micah said (Ezekiel 34:11ff; Micah 5:2; Matthew 3:6), from the town governed by the typologically significant 'shepherd', David.

Placed in a manger, born in a cave or cattle stall beneath an ordinary house, visited by humble shepherds: these were all signs that Jesus was the outsider from the start. However, he was an outsider who knew better than the most well-educated religious insiders what was at the heart of Jewish faith and worship. To see this, we turn to Jesus' presentation and later meeting with the religious leaders whom he cross-examined in the Temple.

## Jesus and the Temple

The final part of the nativity and infancy account in Luke is all about Jesus' reception in, and relationship with, the Temple. Two narratives are placed back to back. The presentation of Jesus in the Temple, which coincided with Mary's purification following childbirth (Luke 2:22–40), precedes a much later story when Jesus was twelve years old (2:42) when he lingers in the Temple "listening to the Temple teachers and asking then questions" (2:46).

Following Jesus' circumcision, which occurred presumably in Bethlehem following his birth (2:21), Mary went up to the Temple in Jerusalem after thirty-three days for her own purification or cleansing following childbirth. This was in accordance with Mosaic law (see Leviticus 12:1–8). Whilst doing this, Jesus was also presented for service to God in the Temple. This action of presentation is reminiscent of the presentation of Samuel to the Lord in the tabernacle at Shiloh (1 Samuel 1:28). However, in the case of Jesus' presentation, two individuals, Simeon and Anna, who had been praying for the redemption of Israel, were miraculously present at the very moment of Jesus' appearance in the Temple. Seeing the child of only forty days old, they prophetically gave thanks for the salvation of God promised in the life of Jesus. The Holy Spirit was strongly present in both Simeon and Anna (see Luke 2:25–27 and 2:38), orchestrating their presence in the Temple at the right moment to see Jesus and bear witness to his role in bringing salvation to Israel. Simeon could die in peace having seen the Christ who would be "a light for revelation to the Gentiles and for the glory to your people Israel" (2:32). Anna, an elderly woman with intercessory and prophetic gifts, likewise recognised Jesus as the one who would bring redemption to Jerusalem (2:38). It must have been a striking sight, this small baby in Herod's massive Temple being praised as the salvation of Israel and the Gentiles. In time Christ would come to replace the Temple. His life and self-offering would make its sacrificial system obsolete, and his body, the Church would replace its ritual and ceremonies in a new fellowship guided and indwelt by the Spirit.

More than anything else, the next story shows this outsider beginning to flex his spiritual authority in such a way that prefigures his eventual replacement of the Temple. This second account, relating events which occurred approximately twelve years later, begins with Jesus' separation from his parents in the throng of pilgrims that crowded Jerusalem for Passover. Having realised that he was not with their party of family and friends from Nazareth, Mary and Joseph returned to Jerusalem to search for Jesus. After searching for three days, they eventually found him in the Temple. They were anxious and no doubt a little cross. By contrast, he appears serene and even a little surprised: "Didn't you know I had to be in my Father's house?" (2:49). His dawning consciousness of divine birthright had emerged. In their turn, the teachers in the Temple "were amazed at his understanding and answers" (2:47). He had been listening and asking questions of the teachers who quickly realised he was no ordinary boy. They were absolutely the insiders: trained in the rabbinic schools, or scribes or Pharisees, many if not all were also priests. Jesus, by contrast, was from a rather despised town in Galilee ("Can anything good come out of Nazareth?", John 1:46). As so often would be said in the Gospels, "where did he get all this learning?".

Conceived outside marriage, born to a young woman in a cattle stall, placed in a manger, visited by shepherds and wise men, from an artisan family in an unprepossessing town in Galilee, heralded by angels, Jesus came to the centre of Judaism expressed in the power of Herod's Temple. He was welcomed by an old and infirm couple directed by the Spirit, and twelve years later, in the same place, he outshone the scholars with his knowledge and insight. The outsider had come to the heart of Judaism. In just a few more years, his manifesto, proclaimed in his hometown synagogue, would electrify and provoke.

CHAPTER 2

# The Manifesto at Nazareth

Most politicians set out their stall by issuing a manifesto. "It's all in our manifesto!", comes of the cry of the politician; "it was not in your manifesto!" comes the cry of a bewildered electorate about a policy for which they did not vote. The manifesto sets out to the watching world what a person or party seeking office hopes to deliver. Invariably, they find it harder to achieve once in power.

Jesus was not seeking office, but he needed to announce what he had come to do because he had come to inaugurate something completely different. It did not depend on his having any political office, but rather on having the support of his followers and the authority of his Father.

Luke carefully sets out the political and spiritual context to Jesus' ministry. Like all the Gospel writers, Matthew in particular, Luke moves his narrative swiftly to the opening of Jesus' public ministry. He is careful to set this beginning in its full imperial, political, and historical context. John received the word of God in the desert (Luke 3:2) in the fifteenth year of Tiberius Caesar, during the local administration of Herod the Great's children (Herod Antipater and Philip, the sons of Herod the Great and Cleopatra of Jerusalem) and a further unrelated Lysinias, as well as Pontius Pilate and the High Priests Annas and Caiaphas. All the Gospel writers agree that Jesus' public ministry began with his baptism by John the Baptist (Mathew 3:13–17; Mark 1:9–13; Luke 3:21–22; John 1:29–34). Luke has already demonstrated the closeness of John to his cousin Jesus by interweaving the narratives of their births. Their parents recognised the intervention of God in their conception, both prophesied over their children when still in the womb or at circumcision (Luke 2:46–79), and their mothers spent time with each other during their pregnancies (1:39ff). Luke gives a little more space to the ministry of John the Baptist. He describes John's preaching (3:1–20) as a call to repentance and preparation, as a call to just and compassionate living, and finally as an anticipation of Jesus' coming who will "baptise you with the Holy Spirit and with fire" (3:16). Despite the challenge of the Baptist's message, which included this call to repentance to a just and compassionate life (see 3:11, 13, 14), Luke regarded his message as one of "good news" (3:18). Not only was it a preparation for the coming of Jesus, his preaching also provided an opportunity for change for the better.

Aged about 30 (3:23), Jesus arrived at the Jordan river where he was baptised, thereby identifying with humanity whom he had come to liberate. Assured by the Father of his sonship ("You are my Son whom I love: with you I am well pleased"; 3:22), he was immeasurably filled with the Spirit who descended upon him in the firm of a dove (3:22). It was at this point in his narrative that Luke chose to introduce the genealogy of Jesus, consisting of seventy-seven generations or names going neatly back to Adam. It is considerably longer than Matthew's forty-one names or generations, and is in reverse order, i.e. from Jesus to Adam, rather than from Abraham to Jesus. Modern scholarship generally concurs with Lord Arthur Hervey, Bishop of Bath and Wells (and while we are on genealogies, my great-great-grandfather!), that Matthew's list "gives the legal line of descendants from David, stating who was heir to the throne in each case, whereas Luke gives the actual descendants of David, in the branch of the family to which Joseph belonged".[19] In any event, Luke's list has a "muddled transmission", though based on some historical material.[20] The purpose of Luke's list "is to stress the universal significance of Jesus for the whole human race, and not merely for the seed of Abraham".[21] Once again, Luke's Gospel emphasises the salvation that Jesus bought for the whole human race.

Announced by John the Baptist, equipped by the Spirit, and assured by his Father's affirmation, Jesus descended from the origins of the human family with which, in baptism, he completely identified. He is subsequently thrust out into the desert by the Spirit for testing. The temptations that Jesus underwent were peculiar to his calling and identity. He did not need to use his power to relieve his hunger after a forty-day fast and thereby prove that he was the Son of God by turning stones into warmly baked bread (4:3). He did not need to gain authority and power on earth by yielding his allegiance, indeed worship, to Satan (4:5–8). He would gain such authority by obedience to the Father and through his redemptive suffering on the cross (Philippians 2:8–11). Nor did he need to gain glory and fame by a trick, like jumping from the pinnacle of the Temple. He would be glorious but by another route, another way (Luke 4:9–12); that is, through the sacrifice of the cross and the triumph of the resurrection. Having repulsed the blandishments of the devil, Jesus returned "in the power of the Spirit" to Galilee (4:14), and to his home town of Nazareth.

## Nazareth

Nazareth does not appear to have had a good press in New Testament times. By the standards of standards of biblical antiquity, Nazareth was relatively recently founded. The settlement of the town took place in the second century BC, probably when Aristolubus II, the Maccabean, conquered Galilee and Judaized it.[22] Galilee, and therefore Nazareth, was caught up in the political and military struggles between the Greek Seleucid rulers and the Jewish revolt led by Judas Maccabeus in 143 BC. For a while this Jewish government ruled unhindered by the Seleucids in Galilee as the former Greek rule crumbled and fragmented in the area. Deeply influenced by Jewish nationalism provoked by earlier Greek rulers, especially Antiochus Epiphanes, the area became a hotbed of patriotism and aspiration to Jewish independence. So "Galilee of the nations" became more overtly colonised by the Jews during the period from 163–63 BC, after which point the Romans, through the victories of Pompey, took charge in the area.

If a period of conservative Jewish colonisation occurred during this period in Galilee and in towns like Nazareth, this set the tone for the type of communities they were, especially in northern Galilee. If we can say that Nazareth was a colonial enclave in which Jewish settlers had established themselves in recent years, then we can imagine that, like any ex-patriot community, they would be intensely nationalistic and religiously self-conscious.[23] If this was the case for the community at Nazareth then it would explain, to some degree, the reaction in the Synagogue the day that Jesus announced his manifesto for his ministry in Israel.

## The Text for the Day

Returning from his forty-day fast in the power of the Spirit, having vanquished his opponent Satan in the trial of the temptations, and having been assured and equipped at his Baptism, Jesus came to the synagogue that Sabbath intent on announcing the scope and character of his mission. Jesus was presumably well-known in his village having worked there for at least fifteen years as a carpenter. However, though they knew him as a carpenter and as a member of local family, Jesus' popularity and claim to being an exceptional teacher was growing. Luke simply tells us that Jesus taught in the synagogues of the area and "everyone praised him" (4:15b), but would it be the same in his hometown?

One Sabbath, after his return from the wilderness, he entered his home synagogue at Nazareth. He was handed the scroll of the prophet Isaiah to read, either at his own request, by the choice of the attendant, or according to the lectionary. He unrolled the long scroll, finding its sixty-first chapter, and read its opening verses. The reading from the prophets normally followed the recitation of the *Shema* and a reading from the Pentateuch.[24] However, Bailey argues that there may have been shock in the synagogue because Jesus did not read the whole passage from these opening verses of Isaiah 61 *verbatim*.[25] The record we have in Luke, if complete, shows that parts of the text were omitted and others were added. There was no mention of the Lord's servant "binding up the broken-hearted" (Isaiah 61:1b), a verse from Isaiah 58:6 was added (to set the oppressed free) and a final part of the proclamation of the Jubilee year was omitted, namely the proclamation of the "day of the Lord's vengeance" (61:2a). Taken as a whole these omissions and addition could together have given the impression to this conservative, ex-patriot congregation living near the Gentile bad lands that God's message of support and solidarity with his people was less solid than they were given to believe from a *verbatim* reading of the Isaiah 61. Indeed, they may have been offended that these verses were deliberately omitted by Jesus, if they really were. It may have seemed that Jesus' inference from this selective reading was that compassion towards his people stopped short of the broken-hearted Jew, or that those who were oppressed by these new settlements were likely to be set free and there would be no vengeance on Israel's enemies as part of the Jubilee, only favour and mercy. Bailey goes on to argue, based on Joachim Jeremias, that the Greek for "all spoke well of him" could equally be rendered "all witnessed against him" and "were amazed at the words of mercy that came from his lips".[26] The point is that the ire of the congregation that day was provoked by their own local "boy from Nazareth" using the scriptures to advocate a merciful policy towards the outsider, the Gentile: the very people whose land they has taken on the grounds of God's favour towards them. A modern equivalent would be an Afrikaner preacher, in a deeply Afrikaner area, urging the acceptance of black communities on equal terms as joint heirs of God's privileges and grace within their territory. Such a view was more than could be taken by the synagogue congregation, many of whom may have been very conservative and blinkered in their understanding.[27]

The more usual interpretation of this incident is that Jesus was giving a general introduction to his forthcoming ministry which would bring freedom, enlightenment, and mercy to all, and that he was the fulfilment which Isaiah had prophesied. The quotation from Isaiah was not so much a coded re-construction of the prophet set to antagonise a conservative congregation, but rather a conflation by Luke of passages often quoted by Jesus to define his ministry, which he initiated here. This interpretation demonstrates that there was a change in the mood of the congregation in Nazareth, from fascination as to who this local carpenter turned religious leader and celebrity was, to outright hostility towards him by the townspeople, so much so that they wanted his death (Luke 4:29). This change of mood came about after the reading of the prophet Isaiah, and may have occurred not so much as a result of the reading itself, but of the claim that Jesus made at the end of it, in which he said Isaiah's words would be fulfilled by his own words and actions.

Firstly then we must look at the claim that Jesus made at the end of the reading.

We are told that having handed back the scroll the attendant, Jesus "sat down" (4:20) and began to teach. Rabbis or teachers sat down to teach. Luke then says "he began by saying", implying that he said much beside, but that the main thing he said was "Today, this scripture is fulfilled in your hearing" (4:21). Here are the opening words of Jesus' public ministry, and what he is saying is that what was promised by the prophet had been, and was being, fulfilled. Here he promises to do what the prophet said: preach good news to the poor, proclaim freedom to the captives, recovery of sight to the blind, and release to the oppressed. Indeed, when his ministry had been underway for a little while and the imprisoned John the Baptist asks for reassurance that Jesus really is the Christ, Jesus replies in a similar vein: "the blind receive their sight, the lame walk, those who have leprosy are cured, the deaf hear, the dead are raised, and the good news is preached to the poor" (7:22). Once again there is a conscious or unconscious fulfilment of Isaiah 61.[28] But what was more shocking or provoking for the people of Nazareth in the synagogue that day was that Jesus had claimed that the opening lines of the prophecy were true of him. "The Spirit of the Lord", said Jesus, was on him "because he has anointed me" (4:18). Since the general Jewish expectation was that the Messiah would have the full anointing of God by the Spirit, here was a Messianic claim for those in the synagogue to contemplate. The fact that they were aware of this accounted for the next part of the response, which is all about Jesus' identity.

The synagogue thought that they knew who he was—"Isn't this Joseph's son?" (4:22b)—and they were struck by his gracious words, but Jesus presses them, and it seems that a beginning of a reaction sets in. He says, "Surely you will say: 'physician heal yourself', in other words, 'do here in your home town what we have heard you do in Capernaum.'" (4:23). However, in his hometown Jesus was less free to act in the Messianic fashion he described because people in Nazareth could not get beyond regarding him as the local carpenter and as the son of Mary and Joseph. Their very familiarity with the Jesus-they-thought-they-knew placed a restriction on their expectations of him, and similarly on his own freedom to act. The other synoptic gospels concur. Mark records more or less the same incident where the very familiarity of the people in Nazareth with Jesus made it difficult for them to have faith in him as the Messiah, or to give him opportunity through their faith in him for him to act as the Messiah (Mark 6:5). "'Isn't this the carpenter? Isn't this Mary's son and the brother of James, Joseph, Judas and Simon? Aren't his sisters here with us?' And they took offence at him" (Mark 6:2–3). It is one thing for someone whom you have hardly met to claim great status or influence for themselves, but when such a claim comes from someone you have known their entire lives, faith and credulity can be strained. This is the disadvantage of the insider compared to the fresh eyes, open heart, and unencumbered knowledge of the outsider. The outsider embraces; the insider remains doubtful. It is to those people, not least the Gentiles, to whom Jesus will go—and he now says as much, pouring fuel on the fire of insider opprobrium.

The turning point in the mood of the synagogue seemed to occur after Jesus' response to their marvelling at his claim that he would *not* be honoured in his hometown. He anticipated that they would want him to do what he had done in Capernaum (Luke 4:23), even though what Jesus did in Capernaum did not lead to their repentance (see Matthew 11:23ff). But when Jesus went on to say that "no prophet is accepted in his home town", the mood appears to change. At first, the synagogue had to face the idea that Jesus was not simply the carpenter's son, one of several brothers and sisters, but that he claimed to be the fulfilment of Isaiah's words about the Messiah. But then within the space of a few minutes they were told that he would not be accepted by them and that they would never see in Nazareth what he had already done elsewhere, for instance in the lakeside town of Capernaum, because of their rejection of him. All in the space of a few minutes, Jesus had made an audacious claim to be the fulfilment of Isaiah's messianic prophecy, which if not true was little short of blasphemy. He then had predicted that he would not be accepted and so consequently would not be able to perform any "works" there. There was a roller coaster of reactions in the congregation: resentment at Jesus' claims, confusion about his true identity, and lastly a sense of offence at his prediction of their rejection. And, in a very real way, this jumble of emotions was self-fulfilling. The very thing Jesus accused them of—not accepting who he was—led inevitably to their rejection of him. But Jesus

went further. Because this conservative border community in a recently
settled area of Galilee could not countenance his being the Messiah, Jesus
told them that, like Elijah, he would go elsewhere, outside Israel. Insult
seemed to be added to injury.

The illustration from the life and ministry of Elijah was pertinent (Luke
4:25–27). Three and a half years of drought and famine had ensued as a
result of Elijah's prayer for the heavens to be closed (1 Kings 17:1). It was
not just a question of a hose pipe ban in the gardens of Israelites but a
failure of crops, and destitution with the weak and vulnerable. As Jesus
said, there were many widows in great need in Israel, but Elijah was sent to
a widow outside Israel in Zarephath (1 Kings 17:7ff), near Tyre and Sidon.
In other words the prophet himself went outside Israel, turning his back
on his own land and people in judgement upon them, and gave succour to
this widow. Likewise, Naaman, a leper from Syria, was healed rather than
any of the lepers in Israel (2 Kings 5:1ff). The point was unmistakeable
to the listeners in the synagogue that day in Nazareth: God would turn
to those outside Nazareth and Israel since they would not recognise or
receive their promised Messiah. This further enraged the townspeople,
who although at first amazed at Jesus' claim to fulfil the prophecy of Isaiah,
were now incensed that they were to be overlooked because they would
not welcome this Jesus, this boy-next–door, as their Messiah. They tried
to kill Jesus by throwing him off a nearby cliff, but either miraculously or
through his own authority or strength he escaped (Luke 4:28–30). What
had begun so promisingly ended in a rejection, which foreshadowed the
wider rejection of Jesus by Israel about three years later.

Nevertheless Jesus had declared his manifesto in his hometown. The
work had begun, the fulfilment of all that had been promised by the
prophet Isaiah was beginning, the Kingdom with the King at its centre
was now here. In its wake the Kingdom would bring restoration, good
news, healing, and freedom: the year of the Lord's favour had begun. This
kingdom would not be received by Israel, at least not by its leaders, but
it would be received by the poor, the excluded, many women, and many
outsiders. It is to that dynamic that we must now turn.

CHAPTER 3

# Encounters with Outsiders

Luke's Gospel devotes consistent attention to encounters between Jesus and outsiders: people who were not part of the religious Jewish community, and who were excluded from the community by virtue of disease, ethnicity, immorality, or occupation. Jesus seems to meet them and minister to them on almost every page of the Gospel, beginning with the leper who sought healing from him at the beginning of his ministry (5:12ff). Jesus freely healed him, and, by getting him to register his cure with the Priest as Moses commanded (5:14), he was once again included in the community. The man needed to be cured but he also needed to be re-admitted into the life of the community, no longer a pitiable outsider whom people at best ignored or at worst fled from. The outsider became the insider through Jesus' ministry. And, contrastingly, the insiders—the Priests, Levites, Pharisees, Sadducees, and Teachers of the Law—who regarded themselves as the guardians of the life of the nation and in touch with God by virtue of their observance of Torah were frequently to become the outsiders. For the spiritual economy of the Kingdom was such that the last becomes first, the least becomes the greatest, and the outsider becomes the insider, and *vice versa*. It is time to meet some of these outsiders and witness their inclusion into the kingdom of God.

## An Encounter with a Paralytic (Luke 5:17–26)

Often the view of the sick and diseased amongst the Jews was that they had brought their sickness or disease upon themselves. It was a natural question for the disciples about the man born blind, "Rabbi, who sinned, this man or his parents that he was born blind?" (John 9:1). It was also the general standpoint of Job's comforters: Job was being punished for his sins. Although in the case of Job and the blind man there was no connection between their life and their afflictions, in this case of the paralysed man, there appears to have been some connection between his lifestyle and his state, as we shall see.

The paralysed man of Luke 5 was quite literally an outsider, since his friends who were bringing him to Jesus could not even enter the house where Jesus was, so great was the crush. The paralysed man was in danger of being left on the outside and consequently not healed. But his friends, who were both ingenious and full of faith, peeled back the tiles on the roof, creating a space through which they could lower the man right in front of Jesus. This vivid and resourceful action gained Jesus' approval: "Friend", he said to the man, "your sins are forgiven" (5:20). With this statement a whole new dimension was introduced to this healing. Jesus not only linked the man's healing to the forgiveness of sins, but in saying that his sins were forgiven he claimed the divine prerogative of absolution. Jesus might have heard no more about this but for the fact that the censorious Pharisees were there in force. It was the clash of two kingdoms, two outlooks, and two dynamics; one sterile and burdensome and the other renewing. The result of this was an illuminating exchange: a clash between Law and grace, mercy and punishment.

Luke describes it as a kind of theatrical showdown between the champion of the outsiders, Jesus, and the insiders (the self-appointed guardians of Torah), the Pharisees. There must have been quite a number of these Teachers of the Law who had come together to appraise this unknown rabbi from Galilee who was drawing so much attention. What we have here then is a confrontation not unlike the one in the synagogue in Nazareth although on different grounds. There, in Nazareth, Jesus shocked the deeply held conservatism of his hearers, firstly by his claim to be the Messiah (when to them he was the boy-down-the-road), and secondly by his intention of bringing salvation outside the borders of Israel. But here, in Capernaum, he shocked the Pharisees by his claim to have power to forgive sins, which was the right of God alone.

But we also have a fundamental clash about how to restore Israel or free her from her exile and domination by foreign power, and give her back her destiny, role, and future. The Pharisees sought to do this by an ever more intense observation of the Torah, following the initiative of Ezra at the time of the Restoration. But in reality this brought only pride, deception, and a burden (11:37–54). For Jesus, the Pharisees in their teaching had "taken away the key to knowledge" they had not entered themselves and "hindered those who were entering" (presumably the Kingdom; 11.52). Jesus, through his power to heal and speak truth, was bringing the Kingdom close to his people. The principal way of opening the Kingdom to the outsiders, and indeed all people, was through forgiveness. So we have the first unambiguous statement in the Gospel that Jesus as the Son of Man—the majestic and powerful figure from Daniel—was empowered not only to heal but also to forgive sins. In fact, in Jesus' argument, his power to heal this paralysed man was the outward and visible proof of his equal power to forgive or heal: for Jesus said, "which is easier to say, 'Your sins are forgiven' or to say, 'Get up and walk'? But that you may know that the Son of man has authority on earth to forgive he who sins" (5:23–24). He could heal, he could forgive, and in the case of this man he did both. The paralysed man who was in danger of being left outside, helpless and frustrated, was first brought inside by the physical action of his friends lowering him through the roof to the feet of Jesus. Jesus then brought him much further in every way *into* the kingdom—and so to come right inside the new order that he was initiating by forgiveness. The kingdom was entered through forgiveness but it was also a place of healing both now and in the future: for as Luke says, "the power he Lord was with him (Jesus) to heal" (5:17b).

## An Encounter with a Centurion (Luke 7:1–10)

Centurions and Roman army commanders tend to get a good press in the New Testament. These commanders of a hundred men, or sergeant majors of the Roman army, were professional soldiers drawn from all over the empire. They were seasoned campaigners, probably good judges of the character of their men, and hopefully, if all went well for them, they would retire and settle down with a pension and a plot of land in some corner of the Empire. But their lives were fraught with danger and retirement might never come, only death on a foreign field that was only temporarily Roman. In addition to the centurion of Luke 7, several well esteemed centurions appear in the gospels: the one who watched Jesus die, the 'commander' who arrested and thereby saved Paul from the mob (Acts 21:31—22:25 ff), and most tellingly, Cornelius in Acts 10. However, the centurion of Luke 7 is not only well thought of by Luke, but by Jesus himself.

There are two points to note in looking at this centurion: both his character and his faith seem to be out of the ordinary, and each is connected to the other. The centurion's character is shown in turn by two actions: his building of the local synagogue for the Jews, and his care of his dying household servant. Although it was well attested that Gentiles often helped with the upkeep of synagogues, to build one was rare.[29] We are told that this centurion loved (7:5) the Jewish people, presumably believing in their God, and had in his own mind come to connect Jesus with YAHWEH as either a prophet or maybe even the Messiah. At any rate, he recognised Jesus' power and authority to heal and, caring for his dying servant, he sent messengers to Jesus (or, in Matthew's version, came himself; Matthew 8:5) to ask for his healing. So we are given a picture of a man who was serious, a seeker after truth and compassionate towards his servant. His integrity and care was linked to a clear-sighted and confident faith in Jesus.

However, the part of the centurion's character for which he is especially known, and for which Jesus unreservedly commended him, was his faith. "Turning to the crowd following him Jesus said, 'I tell you, I have not known such great faith even in Israel'" (7:9). The centurion displays a striking understanding of the status and concomitant authority of Jesus; an insight which, as he himself describes, was based on the similarities he perceived between the working of authority in the Roman army and the working of a greater authority by Christ. "I myself am a man under authority with soldiers under me. I tell this one, 'Go', and he goes: and that one, 'Come', and he comes. I say to my servant, 'Do this', and he does" (7:8). In the army obedience was based on respect, fear, and self-interest, but in Jesus' case the centurion recognised that sickness, disease, and evil were completely obedient to him and submissive to his God-given authority. Whether the centurion recognised Jesus as the Son of God, or God incarnate, we cannot be sure, but his faith was clearly rooted in an understanding and recognition of Jesus' untrammelled authority as "Lord" (7:6). Moreover, all this was from someone who was outside Israel: a lover of the Jews and a patron of their worship, but nonetheless less a Gentile, an outsider. The centurion was another example that this Kingdom, which Jesus brought, knew no bounds.

## An Encounter with a Sinful Woman (Luke 7:36–50)

Jesus' ministry appealed to a remarkable variety of people, from the centurion to the sinful woman to whom we now turn. Later in this book we shall look at Jesus' dealings with women as a whole in St Luke's Gospel, but here we see Jesus encountering a woman in the unlikely setting of a house belonging to a Pharisee named Simon. It is quite probable that the woman was a prostitute.[30] If so, she was a member of one of those professions stringently excluded from Judaism. And she was one of a number of such women whom Jesus met and talked to in the gospels: the woman at the well (if not a prostitute then a serial adulteress), the woman caught in adultery, and possibly Mary Magdalene, although there is nothing definitive said about this. Hearing that Jesus was at Simon's house, this woman deliberately came to see him, bringing with her an alabaster jar of perfume. She came therefore with intent: to thank Jesus, to celebrate and to express her love and devotion to him. Perhaps the likeliest explanation of her actions was that, having heard that Jesus was at the house of Simon and having already met Jesus on some previous occasion when she experienced profound acceptance and forgiveness by him, she came now to express her love and thanks. Arriving at the house where Jesus was dining as a guest of Simon, she was overcome with emotion, wetting his feet with her tears, then "in her anxiety to make up for this mishap, and forgetful of social proprieties, she let down her hair and wiped his feet dry".[31] She then kissed his feet and anointed them with perfume. Simon found this action distasteful and it indicated to him that Jesus did not realise the "type" of woman she was—as far as Simon was concerned, authentic prophets did not associate with prostitutes. But Jesus knew only too well who she was, and how genuine and praiseworthy her actions were.

Jesus begins by putting his thoughts in the form of a parable. Two debtors owed money to a moneylender and were unable to pay. One owed a huge debt of 500 *denarii*; equivalent to over a year's worth of the daily wage of one *denarius*. The other owed the smaller but still significant sum of fifty *denarii*. The moneylender, most uncharacteristically, forgave both debts. Asked which of the two would be most grateful, Simon correctly answered, "the one who had the biggest debt cancelled" (7:43). Then turning to the woman, Jesus praised her actions as indicative of her deep gratitude and love towards him for her forgiveness. Her actions of washing his feet with her tears, wiping them with her hair, kissing them, and then anointing them with perfume were all indicative of her great love and gratitude. Jesus drew the conclusion that someone who knows that they are forgiven much will love much, but those who think there is little to forgive in their lives will love little. Gratitude and devotion, then, are directly connected to the depth and magnitude of our forgiveness.

It is unheard of for a moneylender to forgive such a sizeable debt. Why would he do it? It was an action of pure mercy, grace, and generosity. To forgive is to release a person of any indebtedness or obligation to you; it is to wipe the slate clean of guilt or grudge. Moreover, in the case of either a significant debt or an equivalent failure, it removes the cloud, the constraint and burden that hovers over the person's life. They can live again. The theologian Miroslav Volf tells a story in his book *Free of Charge* of complete forgiveness by his parents of a nanny who was caring for his brother when he died in an accident. He was put on a horse-drawn waggon one fateful day by some playmates in a neighbouring street in

1957. As the wagon passed through a gate on a bumpy cobblestone road, Daniel leaned sideways and his head got stuck between the doorpost and the wagon. The horses kept going! He died on the way to hospital. The nanny, called Aunt Milica by the family, should have looked out for him but she did not. Miroslav's parents never said to him that she was partly responsible. His parents forgave their nanny of any responsibility. They never mentioned it. She gave devoted service to the family for years to come.[32]

In the case of the woman in this story, Jesus very deliberately forgives her. She is already grateful. Already she feels accepted by Jesus, hence her actions. But to make it abundantly plain, he says, "Your sins are forgiven . . . Your faith has saved you; go in peace" (7:48–50). Another outsider, one who felt alienated by her own lifestyle and wrongdoing, is included and forgiven by Jesus.

## The Gerasene Demoniac (Luke 8:26–39)

We have already seen Jesus reaching out to those excluded from society: a leper, a helpless paralysed man completely dependent on his family and friends, and a woman too ashamed to enter into mainstream Jewish society. She too was included. And now the most frightening of all the characters whom Jesus restored, healed, and included: the Gerasene Demoniac.

Jesus was once again ministering on the edges of Jewish society. He had travelled by boat to the south east side of the lake to the region of the Decapolis. The term 'Gerasenes' refers to the inhabitants of Gerasa, modern Jerash or Khersa, where there are some cliffs. There seems to be some textual variation as to the actual name of the place: whether it was Gadara (Matthew 8:28) or Gerasa (Mark 5:1 and Luke 8:26), but whatever the name was, it was in a Gentile region where the farmers kept pigs (unclean animals to the Jews). Here, on stepping ashore, Jesus was confronted by the most tempestuous and frightening character in the gospel, the Gerasene or Gadarene demoniac. Having calmed the storm on the sea while on the way over in the boat (Luke 8:24), here was

another storm, existing internally in an individual, waiting to be calmed
and for the man to be consequently healed. The only way in which the
inhabitants could deal with him was through isolation and restraint. He
was chained hand and foot, kept under guard, roamed solitary places, the
local cemeteries, and was a threat both to himself and the local population.

Even this level of restraint was unreliable, since such was his strength
that he sometimes broke free from his chains (8:29). When Jesus met
him he was isolated, bound, demonised, and dangerous to his keepers: a
man waiting to be freed and calmed. The demons in the man recognised
Jesus, crying out "What do you want with me, Jesus, Son of the Most High
God?" (8:28). They shouted vehemently, which must have been frightening
for most people. But Jesus calmly asked "What is your name?". For Jesus
was there no question of an ensuing tussle to remove the demons from
the man. The demons recognised Jesus' authority over them instantly.
It was not question of *if* they would leave but *how* they would leave,
whether to the Abyss or into the pigs. For some reason Jesus allowed
them to negotiate their destiny with him. They pleaded not be sent to the
Abyss; a kind of subterranean watery deep in Hebrew cosmology, but,
in Revelation, the final place of judgement on all the devil's minions and
works where they are imprisoned and confined for ever (see Revelation
9:1–3, 11; 11:17; 17:8; 20:1–3). Instead, Jesus allows them to go into
the herd of pigs, which then rush headlong into the sea. The reason for
this was not to get rid of the "unclean animals". Rather, this was a more
visible demonstration of Jesus' authority and also the confirmation that
one man's life is more valuable than a herd of pigs. At any rate, the man
was liberated. The villagers were more disturbed by this demonstration
of Jesus' power and the consequent loss to the local economy than the
antics of this preternaturally strong demon-infested man. We are told
that they were frightened by seeing the man "sitting at Jesus' feet, dressed
and in his right mind"; indeed the whole locality was overcome with fear
and Jesus was asked to leave (8:37). Perhaps this is an example of how
the unfamiliar is more fearful that the familiar, however disturbing and
unhealthy the familiar might be. Jesus leaves the region by boat, as he
arrived, and the fully clothed ex-demoniac, now in total possession of
his faculties, has a remarkable story which he feels compelled to recount.
He proved a remarkably effective evangelist, telling the whole town of

his extraordinary transformation. The man who was more of an outsider than any other had been changed, and from now on and from within the Kingdom he told compellingly of the King's authority and power.

## The Oppressed and the Oppressor (Luke 18:35—19:10)

In the last weeks of Jesus' ministry, he went to Jericho (see Luke 18:35, 19:1). Here Jesus had two encounters: firstly, with a man who was oppressed, the blind man Bartimaeus; secondly, with an oppressor, Zacchaeus the tax collector.[33] Both men, for thoroughly different reasons, were ostracised. Bartimaeus because he was blind and a beggar, and almost certainly to Jewish minds because he, or a member of his family, had previously sinned in some way. Zacchaeus because he was an avaricious quisling, working for the Roman imperial power but at the same time making as much money for himself as possible. Both were outside normal Jewish society and their positions showed it: Bartimaeus sat by the roadside begging and Zacchaeus was up a tree with money enough to spare!

These two encounters show the extraordinary inclusiveness of Jesus towards outsiders even during times of great significance and testing in his own life. We are told in Luke's Gospel that Jesus has once again forewarned the disciples of his impending suffering and death: "he [Jesus] will be turned over to the Gentiles. They will mock him, insult him, spit on him, flog him and kill him. On the third day he will rise again" (18:32). Despite these impending events, Jesus' ministry continues in the area around Jericho. The people of the city come out to meet him, thereby according him the status of an important dignitary, and among them is Bartimaeus tagging along. Luke does not give us his name (whereas Mark does, even telling us that he is the son of Timaeus, perhaps known to the first-century Church; Mark 10:46). Luke may have spared us his name because it could be translated as "Son of Filth".[34] Bartimaues waits by the roadside for Jesus to pass by adopting his normal begging position. He asks who is coming. "Jesus of Nazareth", he is told. Interestingly he then calls out "Jesus, son of David have mercy on me", using a title rarely

encountered in the Gospels. It was, in fact, only used otherwise by the
Syro-Phoenician woman (Matthew 15:22).

But the more Bartimaeus cried out, the more he was told to be quiet
by those leading the welcoming party for Jesus (Luke 18:39). For them
Bartimaeus was an embarrassment to be hidden. They did not want Jesus
to be bothered by the likes of him, but Jesus ordered the man to be brought
to him anyway, and then he asked him a curious question: "What do
you want me to do for you?" Given that Bartimaeus was blind, it seems
unnecessary, but was it? The question itself and the asking of it gave him
dignity; after all he addressed him and did not just fling a few *denarii*
into a begging bowl. And it also made Bartimaeaus think: normally he
asked for money hoping for nothing more. Faced with Jesus and knowing
a little about him from the word on the street, he went for the big one:
"Lord I want to see" (18:41). Perhaps he even surprised himself when
he said it: the thing he wanted above all, but dared not ask for, having
contented himself for years that the most he could expect was a few coins
in a begging bowl. For a brief moment his words hung in the air and then
wonderfully Jesus said to him, "Receive your sight: your faith has healed
you". He was a different man.

You would expect Jesus to be on the side of the poor, the marginalised,
and the exploited, but to be on the side of Zacchaeus was something else.
After all, in the words of Mary, "the rich he has sent empty away" whereas
"the hungry were filled with good things" (1:53). But this rich man was
not to be sent away empty, although the weight of the coins in his pocket
or bank balance would be less. He was generously received. There were
outsiders who had been marginalised by their poverty but there were also
rich men who had been marginalised by their wealth, and more importantly
how they obtained it, and that was, in part, what drove Zacchaeus up a
tree. He was short. He was notoriously unpopular as an extortionate tax
collector. He was a collaborator. He was despised. But he was not beyond
the reach of Jesus or the transforming power of his mercy. "Zacchaeus,
come down immediately. I must stay at your house today" (19:5), Jesus
said looking up to him in the tree where he was uncomfortably sitting.
He came down astonished at his good fortune and gladly welcomed him,
while the people complained that Jesus had gone to the house of a sinner
(19:7). The effect of Jesus' presence in his home and life is well known: he

gave half of his wealth away to the poor and promised to pay back four times anyone whom he had cheated. It was a response of deep gratitude for the salvation that had come to him (19:9). The sinful woman washed the feet of Jesus with her tears and wiped then with her hair; Zacchaeus washed the feet of the poor with his money and the hearts of the cheated with his generosity. The means of showing gratitude for acceptance were different; the feelings and attitude expressed was the same.

In these encounters Jesus demonstrated his heart for the outsiders, whether leper, paralysed man, centurion, sinful woman, or demoniac; whether the oppressed or the oppressor. After all, as he himself said, "The Son of Man came to seek and save the lost" (19:10). What Jesus showed in these encounters he also taught vividly and provocatively in his parables; they too had a principal focus in the welcome and love of the outsider.

# CHAPTER FOUR

# The parables and Outsiders

In many ways Luke's Gospel can be described as the gospel of the parable. As Plummer points out,

> Of the twenty miracles recorded by Luke, six are peculiar to him. While, out of the twenty-three parables, all but five are peculiar to him. And he omits only eleven, ten peculiar to Matthew and one peculiar to Mark.
>
> *The parable of the growing seed, Mark 4:26–29*

He goes on to say that Luke uniquely records eighteen parables; i.e. none of these eighteen appear in either of the other synoptic gospels.[35] Matthew and Luke are the great parable tellers; Mark less so. John eschews all parables, preferring in his gospel either symbols or allegories, which are a form of extended metaphor (such as the Vine in John 15). Or to put it another way, without Luke we would have no parable of the Good Samaritan or the Prodigal Son, or The Pharisee and the Publican or the Friend at Midnight, or a further fourteen parables!

The question arises of where Luke obtained these parables which neither Mark nor Matthew include. If there was a source called the "Oracles of Jesus", was Luke alone aware of it and did he hear about this cache of parables whilst researching for his Gospel while Paul was imprisoned in Caesarea awaiting trial (see Acts 23–27, especially 24:27)? For it seems the gospel quite probably was written during that period. Equally, if Luke knew Matthew's Gospel, why did he omit ten of the parables found in Matthew? As Plummer notes,

It should be noticed that most of the twenty miracles in
Luke are in the other two also, whereas only three of the
twenty-three parables in Luke are also in Matthew.[36]

This may mean that they shared a common source for miracles but separate
sources for parables. Or again, Luke may have been familiar with Matthew
and Mark, but neither Mark nor Matthew with Luke. On the one hand,
we can conclude that the narratives of the synoptic gospels are much the
same, with the inclusion of most of the miracles in the same sequence in
each Gospel. But, on the other hand, there is a much greater diversity in
the range of parables used by the synoptic writers, with Luke and Matthew
having more parables unique to them but with Luke having the most.

We could ask the question, why was Luke so partial to the inclusion of
the parables in his gospel? Is it that their use is central to the purpose of
his gospel? Since one of the main purposes of the gospel is the explanation
of the reality and activity of the Kingdom to those who were *outside,*
and since the *raison d'être* of parables was teaching spiritual truth about
the Kingdom to the crowds (Mark 4:33–34), Luke understandably used
them to demonstrate Jesus' ministry to the outsider. It is, therefore, no
surprise that Luke included more parables than any other gospel writer,
and several of the parables are designed to teach, emphasise, and underline
God's grace to the outsider. Many of these parables are unique to him;
the most significant being, the Good Samaritan, the Prodigal Son, the
Pharisee and the Tax Collector. The parable of the Wedding Feast, another
important parable, is shared with Matthew (Matthew 22:1–14). We will
look at these in turn.

## The Parable of the Good Samaritan (Luke 10:25–37)

The two parables that have passed into common knowledge more than any others are the parables of the Good Samaritan and the Prodigal Son. People speak of being "a good Samaritan" or being like the prodigal son. And it is inconceivable to think of Jesus' teaching without thinking of these two stories. We will consider the Parable of the Good Samaritan first.

The context for this parable is worth noting. It is placed in the second half of the gospel after Jesus "resolutely set out for Jerusalem" (9:51). The next part of the gospel is therefore set in the context of a journey towards Jerusalem and the eventual suffering, passion, crucifixion, and victory in resurrection of Jesus. Luke favours the motif of a journey as the thread around which the narrative of Jesus' life and mission develops: just as in the post-resurrection narrative, it is the journey to Emmaus that provides the context for Jesus' most vivid revelation of himself as the resurrected Lord. On this first journey to Jerusalem, Jesus was immediately confronted by the Samaritan opposition, which ironically showed the same antipathy to Jesus and his disciples as to any other Jew. The Samaritans' normal antipathy towards the Jews was enflamed by Jesus' intention of travelling through their territory to the capital they despised (9:53). Jesus tells his disciples not to meet Samaritan hatred with their own when James and John suggest "calling down fire from heaven to destroy them" (9:54). Jesus rebuked James and John, and instead the disciples simply moved on to a more receptive place. But as they walked along, Jesus took the opportunity of telling them of the cost of discipleship and of the inevitability of opposition. It is after sending out the seventy-two (to which we shall return in Chapter 7) that the parable of the Good Samaritan appears, soon after the account of the Samaritan opposition. Despite this, Jesus makes the Good Samaritan the hero of his parable: in other words, Jesus avoids stereotyping the Samaritans as unequivocally bad. Indeed he shockingly applauds the Good Samaritan rather than the Jewish establishment of Priests and Levites. In fact all three of the religious orders in Judaism are involved in this parable. A scribe or expert in the law asks the question—which then precipitates the parable as an answer—while both a priest and Levite appear in the parable itself. The priests are the descendants of Aaron, and the Levites are the tribe assigned to assist the priesthood and keep the Tabernacle and then the Temple (see Numbers 15). The scribes or lawyers were those trained in the Rabbinic schools and from whom the Pharisees were often drawn.[37] The lawyer tests Jesus by asking "what must I do to inherit eternal life?", which Jesus then got him to answer himself, in fact quite rightly. It is the lawyer who then correctly replied that the way to live is "to love the Lord your God with all your heart and all your soul and with all your strength and with all your mind" and "love your neighbour as yourself". The supplementary question "who is my neighbour" (10:25ff) leads to Jesus' recounting the parable of the Good Samaritan.

In this parable, Jesus is explaining the extent of neighbourliness, or caring for and loving others. Are we to love those of our own kind only, or does our responsibility to care extend beyond our own family, class, race, or nation, even to our enemies? The parable is designed to answer that question and so show the true path of discipleship.[38] In the parable, the hearers or crowd would have been expecting a triadic form; that is, the introduction of three characters who reacted in different ways to the event in the story. The failure of the priest or Levite to help would have fuelled the expectation that a third Israelite, maybe a layman, would have come to the man's rescue.[39] The priest or Levite may have been constrained by religious rules from not touching what they thought was a dead man. On the wrong assumption that the victim was already dead they may consequently "have passed by on the other side" (10:31–32). But the crowd would have fully expected the third figure in the story to be one of their kind, a Jew, who would help the man in his need, uncluttered by restrictive religious observance like the Priest and the Levite

The introduction of a Samaritan hero was no doubt provocative, "for Jews do not associate with Samaritans" (John 4:9). Moreover, Jesus then forced the clear-sighted but fastidious lawyer to pronounce that it was the Good Samaritan who acted in a neighbourly way to the victim: going over to him in compassionate care, binding up and treating his wounds, putting him on his donkey, taking him to an inn, and giving generous provision of two days wages for his care (two *denarii*). "Which of these three do you think was neighbour to him?" Jesus asks. Without even mentioning his race, the lawyer says, "the one who had mercy on him" (Luke 10:36–37). The despised Samaritan, the outsider to the Jew, was the one who fulfilled the most Jewish of commandments, "to love our neighbour as ourselves".

## The Prodigal Son (Luke 15: 11–32)

In many ways the Prodigal Son is a misnomer for the parable, for it is a parable about two sons, and the most striking thing about the parable is the generosity of the Father to both of his sons. This parable also originated in response to an objection, voiced in this case by "the righteous", the so-called insiders, that Jesus "welcomes sinners and eats with them" (15:2).

The reason why Jesus associates with such people is simple: God is extraordinarily loving and generous, he puts no moral boundary to his love, and there is great joy in welcoming back any such person into his family or kingdom. The parable of the Prodigal Son falls into two parts. Part one is the story of the younger son and the second part the story of the elder son—the peeved or parsimonious one, certainly not prodigal! In a very real way they depict the outsider (the younger son) and the insider (the older son). Following the narrative order of the parable we will begin with the younger, prodigal son.

The parable of the younger son is a five-part story: he wants, he leaves, he is lost, he returns, and is extravagantly welcomed back. At the outset he wants and asks for his inheritance. As the younger son he is entitled to a third of the father's estate.[40] By bringing forward his inheritance to the lifetime of his father, the younger son was seeking the means of independence. In Middle Eastern culture at the time, it was tantamount to saying to his father, "I wish that you were dead". He is a young man in a hurry, unmarried and therefore probably around twenty years of age.[41] He leaves with his inheritance. It is an offensive act; a rejection of the home and of his father's love. The father's heart is no doubt sad, disappointed, perplexed and anxious for him. He does not resist his son's going though he is wounded by it.

The third part of the story in which the son becomes lost has an air of inevitability about it. The son gathers up all that he has, sets off to a distant land and squanders all that he has in wild living (15:13). And then a famine follows which brings about his degradation. He becomes a swine keeper, he hires himself out, and no one gives him anything. As Henri Nouwen says, the distant country is anywhere where anger, resentment, jealousy, lust, greed, and rivalries take charge. These things quickly transport us into faraway lands; far, that is, from the values of the Father's home, his presence, and his holy love.[42] And when these things take charge, like addictions, a famine follows, most friends turn tail, no one gives us anything, degradation sets in and thoughts turn to what we are missing.

What follows is the long journey home from poverty of all kinds to a totally unexpected and undeserved welcome. This journey began in the prodigal's mind before it ever took place in reality. Firstly, he came to his senses in the far country. He recognised things for what they were: his degradation, his material and spiritual poverty, and his complete lack of a future or hope in his present condition, feeding pods to pigs. In his mind he wearily trudged home with his words of confession on his lips: "Father, I have sinned against heaven and before you. I am no longer worthy to be called your son, make me one of your hired men" (15:19). In Rembrandt's painting the *Return of the Prodigal Son*, the returning son kneeling before his father is presumably a much changed figure: his hair is shaved, his clothes are virtually undergarments, his shoes are worn through, his feet are cut and bruised. The only remaining sign of dignity is the short sword hanging on his hips—the badge of his nobility. Even in the midst of his debasement, he had clung to the truth that he was still "the son of his Father".[43]

But what is entirely unexpected is the welcome. Indeed, before there was a welcome we are told that the father had kept a constant vigil. As Helmut Theilicke says in the title of his book on the parables, God may be characterised as the *Waiting Father*.[44] In fact the father has been looking, searching the horizon and shielding his eyes against the sun to see if his son was returning home. And just as it was unthinkable that a younger son in the Middle East should ask for his inheritance and leave home, so we are told that it was likewise unthinkable that a father should run through the village towards an errant son to welcome him back. For a respected father, breaking into a run was bad enough, but to do so for a son who had squandered everything, which he had so rudely and offensively taken, was beyond comprehension. It was a literally a motion of grace; the father running towards his errant but repentant child. The son recited his well-rehearsed lines of confession, but what he was confronted by was beyond his wildest imaginings: "bring the best robe for him and put it on him. Put a ring on his finger and sandals on his feet. Bring the fattened calf and kill it. Let's have a feast and celebrate". In other words, the father restored his righteousness (the robe), his son-ship (the ring), his dignity (the sandals), and his place in the home (a celebration)—and all this as soon as he came, or nearly reached, home. All this because the father was filled with compassion towards him: this made him run and embrace his son unreservedly. Again as Nouwen writes,

> The true centre of Rembrandt's painting is the hands of the father. On them all the light is concentrated; on them the eyes of the bystanders are focused; in them the mercy becomes flesh; upon them forgiveness, reconciliation and healing come together, and, through them, not only the tired son but also the worn out father find their rest.[45]

If the Prodigal was the obvious outsider welcomed home from the distant land, there was another member of the family much closer to home who was a greater stranger to the true nature of his father's love, although on the outside he looked secure in the home. The elder brother remained on the outside of the celebrations: "he was in field", no doubt diligently working. "He became angry and refused to go in"; his father went out to him to plead with him and reassure him of his love (15:25ff). The elder son is estranged from the home he has never left; although he is with the father he does not know the father's heart. His sense of dislocation is no less profound than that of his errant brother. His journey had not taken him to destitution in which he fed pods to swine and then himself. Rather, it was a more insidious internal journey of the heart whereby his very apparent goodness fed feelings of resentment, envy, and self-pity which were eating him up inside. This spills out in conversation with his father, provoked by the party thrown in celebration of a brother, "who has squandered your property with prostitutes" (15:30). He betrays his inner boiling and festering feelings. He has slaved for his father. He has been obedient, in actions at least, for all his life. He has never had so much as a "goat" to celebrate with his friends. It all comes tumbling out. His very self-righteousness has been the source of his isolation. He has become an outsider in the very bosom of his home.

But the father reaches out to him as well. If on the one hand the father extravagantly welcomes the younger son home, he also assures the elder son, "you are always with me, and everything I have is yours" (15:31). They are both recipients of the father's love. But the question for the elder son is, will he go into the party and celebrate? We do not know. In that sense this part of the parable is left as a challenge. The challenge for the older son is to give up rivalry, resentment, and ingratitude; to recognise what he has and what he has been promised, and to enjoy his home and his brother's homecoming. Whether or not he does is a question that remains to be answered.

This parable of the Prodigal Son or the Father's Love is the longest and most memorable of the three parables with which Jesus answered the objection that he welcomed sinners and ate with them (15:2). The common thread of these parables—the Lost Coin and the Lost Sheep, as well as The Prodigal Son—is that God searches for those who are lost and, when he finds them, he celebrates! His intention is to restore and redeem any who, intentionally or unintentionally, left or wandered away from their true home. Finding them after a search and restoring them to where they belong is a true cause for celebration. The outlook of God therefore is not inwards, towards the ninety-nine sheep or the remaining coins or the older brother. Rather it is outwards to the outsider: the lost sheep, the lost coin, and the prodigal son. But that does not exclude from his care and goodness those who have remained in the fold. In the case of the older brother, he faced the challenge of rejoicing at the welcome home of his younger brother; in the same way the Jews faced the challenge of rejoicing over the inclusion of the Gentiles into God's kingdom.

The two remaining parables that Luke includes in his gospel which demonstrate God's grace to the outsider are the parables of the Pharisee and Tax Collector and of the Great Banquet, a parable that Luke shares with Matthew.

## The Pharisee and the Tax Collector (Luke 18:9–14)

This too, like the parable of the Prodigal Son, would have been a profoundly shocking parable. It contrasts two strikingly different characters who went up to the Temple in Jerusalem to pray; one a very devout Pharisee and the other a tax collector (18:9–14). By implication the tax collector was a collaborator with the Romans, purchasing the right to raise taxes from his fellow Jews. He was expected to make a profit from the tax farming he had purchased. Although taxes may have been fixed by the state, there was great scope for defrauding the public. They were shunned by all respectable people and were on a par with robbers.[46] By contrast, the Pharisee was very devout. He was confident—indeed as Luke said in introducing the parable, he was so self-confident that he despised others (18:9), not least the tax collector who came into the Temple to pray alongside him. Their prayers could have not been more different.

Tellingly, Jesus said the Pharisee prayed *to himself*, meaning that it was not really a prayer at all. It was a paean of self-congratulation in which he praised himself for his religious achievements: he fasted twice a week, he gave a tenth of all he had, and he felt himself to be a cut above "robbers, evildoers and even this tax collector". There might have been a murmur of approval from the crowd as Jesus recounted this Pharisee's worth. By contrast, the tax collector would not even raise his eyes to heaven. He beat his breast and uttered "God, have mercy on me a sinner" (18:13b).

And then Jesus delivered his bombshell. Against all expectation Jesus said it was the tax collector who went away from the Temple "justified" (the Pauline word, used only here in the Gospels, which said that the tax collector was made righteous, that God's righteousness was credited to him although he had none of the Pharisee's conspicuous piety). It was a simply stunning conclusion to this parable. Suddenly, everything was turned upside down: the sinner enters the Kingdom while the Pharisee remains outside; the plea for mercy is more effective than the pleading of religious duties; grace covers over the freely admitted failure of the tax collector, whilst self-satisfied piety cannot bridge the gap between the holiness of God and the boasting spirituality of the Pharisee. For as Jesus explained, "everyone who exalts himself will be humbled, and he who humbles himself will be exalted" (18:14). To put it another way, the insider is left outside and the outsider is brought inside the dwelling of God's salvation. Only one other parable remains to be looked at which a similar reversal which is the parable of the Great Banquet.

## The parable of the Great Banquet (Luke 14:15–24)

The context of this parable is a dinner party given at the house of a "prominent" Pharisee (14:1). Jesus has already given the company a few insights on Kingdom table-manners: not to take the best seats, but to go to the lower ones until called up higher (14:7ff) and to ask people to the banquet who cannot return the favour, such as the poor, the crippled, the lame, and the blind (14:13–14). When a person turns to Jesus and comments with ostensible piety that "blessed is the man who will eat at the feast in the Kingdom of God", he expects the conventional response "Oh that we might keep the law in a precise fashion so that when that great day comes, we will be counted worthy to sit with the Messiah and all true believers at his banquet".[47] However, rather than exchanging pious platitudes, Jesus tells a parable about a Messianic banquet at which the guests are far from ready.

The parable has four parts: the readiness of the banquet, the refusal of the invitation by those who are pre-occupied, the reaction of the master, and the final group of guests. The expectation of a Messianic banquet goes back seven hundred years to Isaiah (see Isaiah 25:6), but with the coming of Jesus the feast is here and those with the "keep the date" invitations are now summoned. But they make excuses. They are preoccupied with land, farming, and a newly married man whose wife who would not have been invited since it was most probably a male only party.[48] As we know, they make excuses, although they have known about the invitation for some time. Their priorities are wrong. They turn down the invitation because of other interests, and it is quite possible, as Kenneth Bailey argues, that the way at least two of them did this (the first and the last) was insulting and offensive to the host.[49] The Master is angry in turn and instructs his servants to invite others who do not have much to be preoccupied with save their own needs—the poor, the blind, and the lame. Where the strong and well-off have declined, the weak and the poor are grateful. They come. Once again it is a question of those who were outsiders being the guests at the Banquet. Nor is it a big step to interpret this parable with Jew and Gentile in mind. The Jews from Moses onwards to the Prophets had received an invitation to this Messianic banquet but, for the most part, they ignored or refused it, so the invitation went elsewhere to the Gentiles and to the despised, immoral, and weak in their community. As we have seen, they were to come and taste the Banquet.

These parables vividly display the dynamic of the Kingdom that Jesus had come to inaugurate. His kingship was a fulfilment of that promised in the Old Testament (see Psalm 72:2, 12–14). It would attract the possessed rather than the powerful, the weak rather than the rich, the outsider rather than the insider, and those who know themselves to be guilty and are ashamed rather than the self-righteous. The parables we have looked at show us all this, but the conversations and encounters in the Gospel also show that there is marked inclusion of women.

CHAPTER 5

# Women as Outsiders

It would be wrong to say that Luke as a Gospel writer had a monopoly of stories connecting Jesus to women; he shares that role with John. After all it is John who gives us the encounter of Jesus with the Woman at the Well, or with the sisters Martha and Mary at the graveside of their brother Lazarus (John 4:1–26, 11:1–44, 20:10–18). Likewise it is John who gives us the account of the woman caught in adultery and most significantly, the meeting of Mary Magdalene with the risen Lord. But alongside John, Luke is the gospel writer who most comprehensively records the responses of women to Jesus, and who builds a feminine response to God's grace through the gospel.

Before turning to the text itself, first we must examine the role of women in Jewish spirituality at the time, their place in Judaism and the way that Jesus dealt with that. In the Old Testament scriptures, much respect and honour is given to the role of women such as Ruth and Esther, and the description of a proverbially good wife in Proverbs 31. From time to time in Israel there were women leaders or prophetesses such as Deborah, Jael, and Miriam. But attitudes to women in the Hellenic period appeared to take a turn for the worse, especially with the writings and influence of Ben Sirach, a scribe from Jerusalem who gained wide acceptance. Written *c.*180–170 BC, his writings have come down as part of the Apocrypha in the form of the book of Ecclesiasticus. The general approach to women in Ben Sirach's writing is suspicious at best and hostile at worst. "Do not put yourself in a woman's hands" he advises, "or she come to dominate you completely" (Ecclesiasticus 9:2; Jerusalem Bible) or "do not dally with a singing girl, in case you get caught by her wiles" (9:4). But later he says,

"A woman's spite changes her appearance and makes her face as grim as a bear's . . . When her husband goes out to dinner with his neighbours, he cannot help heaving bitter sighs" (25:1, 18). Finally pessimism seems to get the better of Ben Sirach when he says of daughters that they are a constant worry to their fathers (a father worries about them marrying or becoming headstrong or not being able to have children—42:9ff). Again of women he says, "Do not sit down with women; for moth comes out of clothes, and women's spite out of woman. Better a man's spite than a woman's kindness: women give rise to shame and reproach" (42:12–14). With this we have reached the nadir of his approach to women, although he has the grace to admit that, "a man who has no wife is aimless and querulous!" and that "the man who takes a wife has the makings of a fortune, a helper to match himself, a pillar of support" (36:24).

If these were some of the prevalent attitudes to women in Judaism during Jesus' time, about 170 years after the writings of Ben Sirach, it is not surprising that women were largely excluded from holding positions of leadership outside the family and educating children in society: in short, they were second class citizens. However, in a number of encounters between Jesus and women in Luke's Gospel, Luke shows Jesus' care of women, the devotion he inspired in them, their significance in the Kingdom, and the deep characteristics of their own feminine response to his grace. We will begin by looking at the freedom he brought to two women deprived of a normal life by a flow of blood and a spirit of infirmity respectively.

## Jesus' restoration of feminine dignity and self-esteem

Judaism was peculiarly sensitive to blood. Blood was the ultimate sign of life, and it was through the shedding of blood that a sacrifice was deemed to have taken place (see Hebrews 9:22). A woman in her monthly menstrual cycle was deemed unclean by virtue of the flow of blood. For a week during and a week after it she was deemed unclean (*niddah*). The man was not to have sexual intercourse with her for two weeks (Leviticus 15:19ff): in the first week, intercourse with a woman would render the man ceremonially unclean (and in Leviticus 20:18 the punishment appears to be more severe, he is to be "cut off from his people"). But the Orthodox Jew might wait a further week. And if the flow of blood should continue beyond the length of her period, then such an issue of blood from a uterine haemorrhage or something similar would render her continually unclean (Leviticus 15:25–27). This meant that anything she touched would become unclean, any furniture or chair or bed. Anyone who touched her or anything she has touched would be unclean as well. It was into this lifestyle of exclusion and abjection that this woman was cast. For twelve years she had lived life like this: a virtual outcast, excluded from worship in the Temple at Jerusalem; unable to join normal family, village, or social gatherings; unable to join the parties going up to Jerusalem for the annual festivals. She was left alone; an outsider, ashamed, unwanted, and quite possibly reviled. Imagine her desperation for healing and restoration. She had spent all her money on doctors but to no avail, and her last desperate idea was to touch Jesus anonymously. One day an opportunity presented itself, as Jesus travelled to visit the house of Jairus, the ruler of the synagogue. Jairus' twelve year old daughter was dangerously ill, and in desperation he threw himself at Jesus' feet, begging him to come to the house. Jairus' daughter died whilst waiting for Jesus (Luke 8:49), who was delayed by the interruption of the woman seeking her own healing. Whilst Jairus' daughter had spent her short life in innocence and childhood amid a respected ruling family, the woman had spent those same twelve years in suffering and shame. But it was about to come to an end.

She said to herself, "If only I could touch the tassel [*kraspedon*] on his garment", for every Jew wore four tassels on the four corners of his outer garment (Numbers 15:38ff and Deuteronomy 22:12). Each tassel had a blue cord symbolising the commandments that the Jew was to keep. To touch a tassel was to touch the mercy and expectation of God, exemplified by these commandments. Her faith was such that she believed that if she could but touch Jesus' garment, she would be made well. She was, but she may not have bargained for what happened next. Jesus stopped immediately and said, "Someone touched me; I know that power has gone out from me" (8:46). He sensed that a spiritual power for healing had left him, and may also have known who touched him and why. He invited her to come forward and make herself known. She was afraid, but she came forward. "Trembling and fell at his feet" and in full view of everyone, she explained "why she had touched him and how she had ben instantly healed" (8:47b). Jesus replied with words of restoration: "Daughter your faith had healed you. Go in peace" (8:48). If the flow of blood had excluded her for twelve years, its healing immediately restored her to the community; she was no longer ritually unclean and could take her place fully in the life of Israel as a daughter of Abraham. With one touch her exclusion was at an end.

Another woman who received healing from Jesus had been crippled for an even longer time. The story of this woman's healing (13:10ff) has a dual emphasis: the woman's release from a crippling condition through the power of the Kingdom *and* the authority of Jesus to give life on the Sabbath. Healings which occurred on the Sabbath were often a cause of conflict with the religious authorities and Pharisees (see also Mark 2:23ff; John 9:13ff). Once again Jesus, through healing, restored this woman to a normal life, after an anything but typical period of eighteen years.

## Five marks of feminine spirituality in Luke

If Luke shows Jesus, as other gospel writers do, restoring the dignity of women, he also shows the qualities of faith demonstrated by women in an almost unique way. There are five marks of feminine spirituality, which Luke shows through stories in his Gospel. We will begin with the visit to Martha and Mary's house in Bethany.

### Attentive listening (Luke 10:38–45)

The relationship of Jesus to Martha, Mary, and Lazarus is well described in the gospels of Luke and John: he is a close friend. John tells us candidly that Jesus loved this family and he may have stayed or ate there frequently (John 11: 5). No mention is made of the parents, and you have the feeling that the family were more or less contemporaries of Jesus; we wo

his peer group. Today they might have shared social media! The occ

that Luke records here may have been early on in their friendship. W

is evident in the story are two strong feminine traits, one of which Jes

especially commends. These traits are to provide hospitality and to give

undivided attention. The former trait spurs countless women to provide

good food, to present a tidy, welcoming home—well decorated and

showing signs of care and thought. The latter trait is to give undivided

attention and care to people, whether dependent children, infirm parents,

needy neighbours, or partners or lovers. The capacity for a woman to

give herself unreservedly for the needs of others is clear throughout life

and throughout history. Translated into the spiritual realm, this trait

produces great intercessors, prophets, or carers: it is quite simply the

ability to give oneself to another. Between them the sisters have both

characteristics in spades.

Martha feels the responsibility of providing the hospitality, of getting

the food, of preparing the meal (in this case for around fifteen people in

all), and of making the guests comfortable. It was a big task especially if

it was done on her own, since Mary would not help. No wonder Martha

felt a little resentful; her sense of responsibility had produced anxiety. She

addressed Jesus, whom she had invited into her house, with the reproachful

words "Lord don't you care that my sister has left me to do all the work

by myself. Tell her to help me" (Luke 10:40b). In short, she exhibited all

the diligence of a woman bent on caring for her guests, but none of the

awareness of what that principal guest could offer her. She was bent on

giving all she had to the point of wearing herself out, whereas her sister

was bent on receiving all she could from Jesus. In response to her plea,

Jesus replied, no doubt challengingly but tenderly, "Martha, Martha, you

are worried and upset about many things, but only one thing is needed.

Mary has chosen what is better, and it will not be taken away from her".

Mary, we are told, had sat at the Lords feet listening—this was the better

part (10:39).

Attentive listening lies at the root of prayer. This was true for Julian

of Norwich, Teresa of Avila, and a committed intercessor with whom I

once shared a house. Their gift of attentive listening to God in intercession

is the true spiritual motor for mission and the heartbeat of worship. It

ıld say

sion

at

s

ꞷꞷ

ꞷrace enacted by Mary of Bethany that was

ı-8)

ᵤuality in prayer commended by Jesus and found in Luke's
ᵤ was persistence. He strongly encouraged such persistence in the
parable of the persistent widow and the unjust judge (18:1–8). Jesus may
have chosen the character of a widow as the central one in this parable
because of their vulnerability to injustice, but also because women can
be well known for their tenacity and resolve, pursuing their cause with
determination and even obstinacy. This is certainly felt by the judge, who
attempted to sidetrack the widow with excuses and prevarication. But the
woman was having none of it, continually coming to him with her cause,
so much so that the Judge thought he would be worn out by her (18:5).
In the end he relented of his inactivity and granted her the justice she
was looking for. Finally her persistent pleas prevailed. And Jesus' point
in the parable was that if the unjust judge heard and acted on the widow's
plea, how much more would a just and loving Father and Judge in heaven
vindicate the righteous (18:7). The woman's persistence was the example
to us to "always pray and not give up"; it was also symbolic of a woman's
response to the challenge of finding justice.

### Sacrificial generosity (Luke 21:1–4)

Although this story (which is also told in Mark 12:41–44) deal with one of
Luke's principal concerns, namely wealth and giving, it centres on a poor
widow. Just as a widow was at the centre of Jesus' parable about persistent
prayer so another widow, one of the most vulnerable members of society,
was at the heart of this act of generosity, and a poor widow at that.

Jesus was seated with his disciples around him in the Temple area near
the Treasury. People made their way there to make their offerings to God.
There were thirteen trumpet-shaped collection boxes next to the Treasury
to receive their gifts, and as the gift was made in front of a Priest both the

amount and the purpose of the gift was called out by the donor, so there was plenty of scope for making an impression.[50] Jesus watched the wealthy make their gifts, no doubt with a flourish and a sense of assurance, when an old, poor widow made her way to the collection point. She put into two *lepta*, Greek coins of small value. Jesus noticed her gift and made the declaration that her gift, in proportion to her overall wealth and in comparison to the others, was worth far more. She had given everything, "out of her poverty she had put in all she had" (Luke 21:4b); whereas the others who were rich had given just a small proportion of their wealth. The poor widow was undoubtedly the faith-hero of the story. A woman who would have been regarded as an outsider to the religious social circles of Jerusalem had given more than all of them put together. Not in literal financial terms, but in the deeper ways in which our giving is measured: in generosity, in faith, in devotion. Once again in Luke's Gospel, a woman outstripped all others when it came to generosity.

**Extravagant adoration (Luke 7:36–50)**

For an example of extravagant adoration we return to the story of the woman in the house of Simon the Pharisee (7:37–38). This woman is one of two who anoint Jesus with costly perfume in the gospels; the other is Mary of Bethany who anoints Jesus shortly before his arrest and passion (John 12:3ff). What is common to both is their action of extravagant adoration of Jesus. In both cases the women came with the intention of anointing Jesus with something precious to them. They had in their possession perfume, which they had no doubt saved for a special moment and which was very valuable. In the case of Mary we are told that it was worth a year's wages (John 12:5b); that is around 300 *denarii* or around £25,000 of today's money. We do not know whether the perfume belonging to the woman in Simon's house was as valuable nor how she came by it; perhaps it was payment for her services or maybe a gift or inheritance from family or friends. All we know was that it was very valuable.

She came deliberately to anoint Jesus as an act of gratitude or thanksgiving. They had presumably met on some previous occasion and she had felt both accepted and forgiven. Hearing that Jesus was in

Simon's house, she came with her alabaster flask of perfume to anoint Jesus in gratitude for her forgiveness. But being overcome with emotion she began to weep, and then, a little embarrassed that she had wet Jesus feet with her tears, she wiped them with her hair. And finally she anointed them with perfume.

Jesus tells Simon the Pharisee that he had not given him such a welcome: neither welcoming him in such a manner, nor washing or kissing his feet, nor anointing him (7:44ff). This woman had done all this because she loved much, and she loved much because she had been forgiven much. But it was also a deeply feminine response. It is not just that she had been freed from having given herself, or been taken advantage of, as a woman in what is called the oldest profession in the world. It is that her response to grace or forgiveness is exceptional. If you were to reflect on the question, what characterised her response in comparison to the response of almost countless others in the Gospels who were healed, helped, or delivered? You would have to say that her response was marked by a combination of deep personal gratitude, profound emotion, spontaneous love, and extraordinary generosity. All of these came together in her response to the sheer lavish grace of Christ which both forgave her entirely and freed her from past. That too can only be because she recognised in Jesus the voice and action of God himself—the God of her people the Jews and her ancestors Abraham, Isaac, and Jacob. In other words, as far as she was concerned, what Jesus said and did for her, God did for her. She understood that God was at work uniquely through Christ: and nothing would shift her from that, it was her salvation!

Furthermore, her actions are a model for our devotion. There is about her action more than a touch of "sober inebriation", which Jean Danielou describes as a characteristic of mystic prayer.[51] The essential nature of this ecstatic devotion is "a going out of oneself, not by unconsciousness involving the suspension of activity, but by a kind of projection of the soul beyond the laws of reason under the impulse of Love".[52] The woman in Simon's house was transported beyond mere reason and she acted under the influence of love: she loved much because she was forgiven much. Like Mary in John's Gospel, she stands as a model of self-giving adoration, in her case compelled by forgiveness. Hers was a uniquely feminine response to God's grace and along with the Virgin Mary—whose response to the news that she would bear the Christ-child in her body was a full surrender of her will to God's—this was the quintessence of faith and of venturesome abandonment.

## Obedient faith (Luke 2: 26–38)

As I write, the third in line to the British throne is about to arrive, to a couple well known worldwide as Kate and William. No birth of an heir has been more heralded, not even that of William himself, born 31 years ago. There was no Internet then, and nothing like the intensity of interest worldwide. The Press are encamped outside the West London Maternity suite where the third in line to the throne will be born. What could be more different to the circumstances of the birth of Jesus nearly two thousand years earlier? No room could be obtained for him; few then knew who it was who was arriving save some shepherds, three Magi from the East, and his parents. No one knew then the course that events would take in the life of this royal personage, the kind of Kingdom to which he was heir, nor the twists and turns of popularity and rejection that he would experience.

At the centre of this narrative was a young woman who faced these events with remarkable serenity, supported as she was—after the intervention of an Angel in a vision—by her husband Joseph. If Mathew tells us the story, for the most part, from the point of view of Joseph, Luke tells us the story from the point of view of Mary.

One phrase in Luke's account sums up her spirituality, her outlook, her serenity, and her obedient faith. It comes after the visit of the Shepherds following the appearance of the angels to them above Bethlehem. The words are both simple and profound: "But Mary treasured up all these things and pondered them in her heart" (2:19). The shepherds returned jubilant to their flocks, Mary by contrast was joyous in a different way. Her interior joy was both a product of earlier faith. On being told that she would bear the Christ-child without normal conception, she believed. But her joy was tinged with seeming restraint compared with the shepherd's simple ebullience. For she knew, intuitively, and would soon know more directly, that her vocation was neither easy nor straightforward. It would only be a few weeks later that the young mother would journey again to Jerusalem. This time *not* for Jesus' circumcision, done on the eighth day possibly in Bethlehem, but for her own purification. And then she was told by Simeon the sobering prophetic words that Jesus would be a child "destined to cause the falling and rising of many Israel" *and* "that a sword will pierce your own soul too" (2:28ff). So there was much for Mary both to treasure and ponder: the first appearance of the Angel Gabriel to her at the annunciation (1:28ff); the reaction of Joseph and his change of heart following a vision (Matthew 1:20ff); the meeting with Elizabeth (1:39ff); the journey to Bethlehem and the birth itself (2:1ff); the coming of the Shepherds and Wise Men (2:8ff; Matthew 2:1ff) and the prophetic words of Simeon. Treasuring and pondering was Mary's way of internalising the extraordinary events that had happened to her, and in this she was also conceived obedient faith, which is nowhere expressed more spontaneously than in her words, "I am the Lord's servant, May it be to me as you have said" (Luke 1:38).

Mary's obedient faith added to the other characteristics of feminine response to grace in Luke makes a formidable witness by women in his Gospel. Taken together with attentive listening (Mary of Bethany), persistence (the widow in Jesus parable about prayer), sacrificial generosity (the widow's mite), and extravagant adoration (the woman in Simon's house) we have qualities, which define the parameters of response to Jesus in any generation. And, by contrast, the men in the Gospel come off badly: disputing as to which of them was the greatest (22:24), deserting at the arrest (22:54), and denying Jesus when under pressure (22:60ff). Luke demonstrated comprehensively that although women may have been regarded as unequal to their male peers in social standing in Israel, in his Gospel, when it came to faith and service, they were peerless.

# CHAPTER 6

# The Gospel and the Poor

Luke's Gospel is sometimes called the gospel for the poor. It is fair to say that there is more in this gospel about the treatment of the poor and the handling of wealth than in any of the others. The point is that salvation affects our attitudes to both wealth and poverty: it is transformational, changing our allegiance to wealth as well as igniting our motivation to give, fuelling our response to the poor. Where neither of these two results occurs, we must question whether salvation has truly come.

The material that Luke gives us in relation to these issues ranges over a variety of literature in the Gospel: there is teaching about the dangers of wealth and the rewards of poverty; there are incidents in which Jesus encounters those who in their lives are either gripped by wealth or dominated by its responsibilities; and there are several parables in which the handling of wealth reveals a person's inner motivation and true spirituality. All this is found in the Gospel and together it forms a substantial amount of Jesus' overall teaching in it. Jesus brings freedom from the power of riches, a genuine concern for the poor or victimised, and proper responsibility both in money's gain and use. We will look at each of these aspects of Luke's anthology on wealth, its uses and misuses, in turn, and do so with a view to seeing Luke's overall ethic on wealth, its opportunities as well as its pitfalls.

## Luke's Ethics Regarding Wealth

Some of Jesus' teachings about the responsibilities of wealth and attitudes to it come in his sermon on the plain, the equivalent of Matthew's Sermon on the Mount. In Luke the same teaching is split over two occasions (see 6:17–49 and 12:22–34).

Speaking to a large crowd drawn from Jerusalem and Judea, as well from Tyre and Sidon, many of whom, we are told, had received healing (6:19), he announced a number of blessings and woes that depict two ways of life which in turn carry contrasting consequences or results in the Kingdom. Jesus begins with those who are blessed: surprisingly to us they are the poor, the hungry, the sorrowful, and those who are hated, reviled, or ostracised for the sake of the Kingdom. In other words, situations or conditions which in the world would look like losing ones, in the Kingdom can be means to real blessings. It is not that their pain is necessarily any the less, but that these experiences—awful in themselves—can be the means of knowing God and his Kingdom more deeply. Speaking recently to a nurse who lost her fiancé in a tragic road accident, the pain of loss, although heart-breaking, has enabled her to care with still greater understanding and unusual compassion for others, as well as quickly assess their pain. Jesus pronounces such people blessed not because the conditions of poverty, hunger, sorrow, or persecution are in any way *good* in themselves but they can become purposeful only in so far as the blessings of God's Kingdom may be experienced even in them.

Contrastingly, those conditions to which most of us aspire, namely being well fed, well entertained, and popular, do not necessarily intrinsically confer blessing (6:24–26). Indeed Jesus goes so far as to pronounce woes on such lifestyles, again not because any of those things are wrong in themselves (there is nothing intrinsically wrong with good food, wealth, good entertainment, or being held in respect and affection by many), but each of them *can* feed our pride, insulate our spirit, and turn our ambition away from seeking God and his Kingdom. So those who make these things their goal in life will end up the loser. They may experience woe; that is, a state of being which is without God's presence. Yes, they may have lots of spending money, access to rich fare and fine wines, have plenty of amusing entertainment, and be verging on being a celebrity, but if it all comes at the expense of not knowing God then to Jesus these pleasures become like a heap of ashes.

Next Jesus gives us his familiar reversal teaching, summed up with the question, "What good will it be for a man if he gains the whole world, yet forfiets his soul?" (Matthew 16:26a). That is, what happens is the reverse of that for which you had hoped, because in possessing the world you forsake the Kingdom. For Jesus, eternal rewards are a present reality and present rewards can too easily obscure eternal realities (see Luke 6:23) as time is kaleidoscope or collapsed in Kingdom chronology. This is a fundamental view of wealth in Jesus' teaching. Likewise we are to treat others and ourselves in precisely the opposite or reverse way to what you would ordinarily expect. So we are "to love (our) enemies and do good to those who hate you, bless those who curse you, pray for those who ill treat you" (6:27–28). And even more, "if someone strikes you on one cheek, turn to him the other also, If someone takes your cloak, do not demand it back" (6:27ff). On the one hand we are to treat people in the way we would not naturally treat them but on the other hand we are "to do others as you would have them do to you" (6:31—the Golden Rule).

But if, on the other hand, we do what is *not* expected—loving enemies, lending to those who cannot repay, inviting to dinner those who cannot invite back—then our eternal reward will be great *and* we will be like our Heavenly Father who is kind to the ungrateful and merciful to the wicked. Furthermore, to be critical of yourself and not judgemental towards others but generous will only result in further blessing (6:36ff).

Jesus' counter-cultural lifestyle has further advantages, which are spelt out later in the Gospel. It replaces anxiety with trust. In his recent book entitled *Affluenza,* the psychologist Oliver James traces a new worldwide disease which he calls *affluenza* which is an infection of our material aspirations.[53] He travels the world meeting severe cases of affluenza in places like New York, Shanghai, Australia, Singapore, Copenhagen, and London. What they all have in common is an infection passed by a virus that craves image, success, celebrity, and ownership. The virus comes about when we confuse what we want with what we truly need. We need emotional and material stability (enough rather than excess) to feel part of a community, to give and receive love from family, neighbours, and friends, we need to feel competent in what we do and contribute, and to a large extent able to direct our lives. If these good aspirations are confused with stoked-up desires for high earning, possession, the right image, and even a celebrity-quest then by replacing needs with wants we have become vulnerable to the fully blown virus *of affluenza*. We could end up like one interviewee who said, "My goal is to keep earning for thirty years, educate the kids, pay for my daughter's wedding, and then die". He was wealthy, sophisticated, and amusing but felt like a hamster on a remorseless and sterile wheel.[54]

As far as Jesus was concerned, although the opportunities for affluenza were much more restricted in the society in which he lived, they were still real. So in the well-known parable of the sower, one of the pressures that crushes the growth of the seed that fell amongst thorns is that they are "choked by life's worries, riches and pleasures, and they do not mature" (8:14). But Jesus goes on to give more extensive teaching about combatting anxiety in relation to material things in a section placed carefully after the parable of the Rich Fool (to which we shall return), where Jesus says, "do not worry" about food or clothing (image) or the span of our life (12:22ff), for worry can improve none of them, anxiety cannot produce food, clothing, or health. The antidote to anxiety is faith exhibited by creation: by the birds or ravens that are fed (and which Luther called "blessed theologians") and by the lilies that neither "toil nor spin" (12:27). Indeed, you could argue that the true outsider when it comes to material things, *in extremis,* was John the Baptist of whom Jesus said to the crowd "What did you go out into the desert to see? A man dressed in fine clothes? No, those who wear fine clothes are in King's palaces" (Matthew 11:7–8). John came wearing clothing made of camel's hair, with a leather belt around his waist and eating locusts and wild honey and "he lived in the desert until he appeared to Israel" (Luke 1:80b).

In the sermon on the plain, and in the additional section in Luke 12:22–34, Jesus gives us part of his teaching about the opportunities, responsibilities, and pitfalls of wealth. He summarises the teaching with the exhortation to, "Sell you possessions and give to the poor, (build) treasure in heaven and not on earth where it will not wear out" and he gives us the spiritual axiom, "Where your treasure is, there your heart will be also" (12:34), but it is in the parables that he lays bare the spiritual issues related to wealth, poverty, and accountability. We shall turn to them now.

## Parables about the Function and
## Responsibilities of Wealth

There are four principal parables that fall into this category. They are the Parable of Dives and Lazarus, the Parable of the Rich Fool, the Parable of the Shrewd Manager (Unjust Steward), and the Parable of the Ten Minas. If there is a single issue that joins these parables together it is the responsibility to make money work justly. Our task will be to define what does it mean to make money work justly; everything is contained in that little word *justly*. A just use of money in society is not that everyone has the same but that everyone uses money responsibly. And to handle money responsibly is to care for the needs of the poor, the disadvantaged, and vulnerable as well as for your own family.

We are in the middle of a national debate about how to make money work in the interests of the community and, in particular, how are the suppliers of money, the banks and government, to do that in the context of an economy that remains at best sluggish and at worst flat-lining. After the Banking Collapse of 2008 a number of principles are hopefully coming home to roost: that banks hold a higher proportion of assets in relation to lending, that a division is made between their retail work and speculative investment side (casino!), that there is greater responsibility in lending, that bonuses do not fuel irresponsible lending or speculation. And with an Archbishop on the Parliamentary Banking Standards Commission, and a strong advocate of Credit Unions, there is a voice for the principles of these parables to be heard in the highest councils of the land. Likewise, with companies which market public utilities such as water, power, gas, and electricity, there is a delicate balance to be struck between profitability and future investment *and* responsible, justified pricing in the wider public interest as well as for shareholders (who most likely are pension funds). It is a difficult circle to square.

But on matters of national expenditure there are also other issues to face: what is the right balance between encouraging people back into work (with the concomitant responsibility of providing jobs through the private and public sector) and making proper provision for those who are genuinely vulnerable and in need of support, without corroding self-respect by paralysing people's initiative through benefit buffering?

How do we care for an ageing population? What level of access to the judiciary do we give through legal aid and what level of defence can we afford in the future? Can we provide a free Health Service for all? With a barely increasing rate of national growth, what principles can we gain from these parables both for our personal and corporate financial life? We shall look at each in turn.

### Dives and Lazarus (Luke 16:19–31)

The context of this parable is a continuing stand-off with the Pharisees over money. Most of the chapter is devoted to teaching about money, apart from some brief remarks about divorce (16:18). After an initial parable about the Shrewd Manager (*aka* the Unjust Steward) to which we shall return later, Jesus makes some general conclusions about money or assets (possibly both spiritual and material ones): if we are faithful over a little we may be entrusted with much (and *vice versa*), and that we cannot serve two masters: God and Money. The Pharisees are then picked out as those who "love money" and whom, it seems, consequently sneer at Jesus (16:14). It is in this context that Jesus goes on to tell the parable of the Rich Man and Lazarus.

The parable, which has a familiar ring to it, may well have it its origins as an Egyptian fable now pressed into service by Jesus with Jewish differences.[55] It might well have been familiar to his hearers, but now it is given fresh and vivid reality by Jesus' retelling it with new twists. He transfers it into a Jewish context with reference to Abraham, and the Law (Moses), and Prophets (16:31). It has a vivid setting. The rich man is dressed in the best purple, an exotic cloth, which in later years, as *porphyry*, was the dress code for the royal family and the Emperor in Byzantium. Purple was the colour of patrician leadership in the Roman Empire, and bishops who became rulers in the Roman provinces in later years took to wearing it as well! The rich Man wore purple and had fine linen under garment too (*bussos*, the Greek word used to describe fine Egyptian cotton). There was a touch of humour in the seriousness here; this rich man wore not only the finest purple to denote his status but fine quality underwear as well![56] He was well dressed and he ate well too, "he lived in luxury every day" (16:19).

At his gate lay Lazarus, the only named character in any of Jesus' parables. The name abbreviates in English the Hebrew *el'azar*, meaning "he whom God helps".[57] The name hints at the piety of this poor man. He could not walk. He was laid at the gate of the rich man. He longed for any food, which fell from the rich man's table, and the dogs licked his wounds. Saliva had healing properties, so the animal world did for him what the human world would not. It took a dog to shame (if shame had been possible) his nearest neighbour.

But mortality or death is a great leveller and, indeed, the justice of God after death brought a great reversal. The poor man was transported by angels to the bosom of Abraham; the rich man to the fires of hell. The rich man craved relief from the heat of hell; the poor man was now separated from him by a great chasm (16:26), which was not navigable. Justice is pronounced by Abraham: the comfortless Lazarus is now comforted, and the more than comfortable rich man has no comfort at all. And the reason for this was the neglect by the rich man of his responsibilities under the Law to the poor. Under the Jewish law care for the poor was mandated (Exodus 23:11); Job, as a righteous man, knew of his responsibility to share his wealth the poor (see Job 29:15ff), and likewise this rich Jewish man knew of his responsibilities but chose to ignore them. Such was his (and people like him, e.g. the Pharisees) hardness of heart that not only would they ignore the statutes of the Law and the warnings of the Prophets but also even should someone return from the dead they would ignore him (16:31)!

It is a powerful parable about the responsibilities of the wealth and speaks across the years to the materialist West and to me today. My food is good as I shop in the supermarket and see the endless shelves of food, the extraordinary choice compared with the few root vegetables and fruits in West or East Africa laid out on the roadside to buy or barter for. My clothes are many, with suits, shirts, and underclothes from which to choose; made very often in India, China, and Korea by labourers with very different lifestyles. Earlier this year many perished in an overcrowded, unsafe factory in Bangladesh; they were producing clothes for the West. News comes across my desk in the form of an appeal for the victims of war in Syria, a country that just a few years ago I visited and enjoyed, but now filled with people with wounds and terrible injuries and unspeakable losses inflicted by violence.

How do I eat? How do I clothe myself? What do I do about the cry of the poor and the dispossessed in this ancient Biblical land? Do I close myself off with my rich food, fine clothes, and no wounds; how do I show my care for the poor? What difference does the Law, the Prophets, and the voice of one Risen from the dead make? But neither Luke nor Jesus leave it at that, there are other parables to follow.

### The Parable of the Rich Fool (Luke 12:13–21)

If the parable of the Rich Man (Dives) and Lazarus vividly highlights the misuse of wealth and the hardness of heart that it can sometimes lead to, as well as the justice of God punishing disregard for his teaching but instead rewarding the faithful poor, the parable of the Rich Fool shows the spiritually blinding effect of prosperity.

Once again Jesus is teaching people by the thousands and in their eagerness to hear him teaching, the crowd are in danger of trampling each other to death (12:1). Jesus, in stark terms, has been saying that "there is nothing concealed that will not be revealed, or hidden that will be made known" (12:2). Spurred on by this a man in the crowd shouts out, "Teacher tell my brother to divide the inheritance with me" (12:13). Jesus will not be drawn into family arbitration but gives the general warning that serves as the introduction to the parable: "Watch out! Be on your guard against all kind of greed; a man's life does not consist in the abundance of his possessions" (12:15). To illustrate this he tells the parable of the Rich Fool.

He is a fool simply because he thinks only of his own material well-being despite the blessing of God and, rather than sharing his surplus—which he does not need—with the poor, the rich fool determines to build bigger barns to simply store it for himself. Once we get to a place where possessions are not used but simply stored we are on dangerous ground. The fool is rich towards himself but not rich towards God (12:21). What drives him is his own ambition, "*I* will tear down my barns and build bigger ones . . . *I* will store all my grain and goods . . . and *I* will say to myself 'take life easy: eat, drink and be merry'. But God said to him 'you fool! This very night your soul will be demanded from you. Then who will get what you have prepared for yourself'" (12:18ff). On his tour of the great cities of the world, Oliver James, in his book *Affluenza,* writes of a meeting with Sam in New York. Living in downtown Manhattan and earning *c.*$20 million a year he seemed eerily insulated in his own world as if there was a layer of cotton wool between him the needs of the others. Deeply affected by a famous and emotionally indifferent father, he was also emotionally damaged in childhood. The effect of this emotional deficit and great wealth made him like the rich fool in the parable. Like him, Sam thought in terms of "eat, drink, and be happy". But being happy was more of a challenge as it was hedged about by fears and neuroses to do with loosing what he had through terrorism, and struggling to be happy because of the emotional cost of his childhood. Nevertheless, increasing his wealth was his main ambition. It was the only measurable aim he had, but it is an aim which is painfully deficient.[58]

Basil of Caesarea, in his burning homily on this parable entitled *I Will Tear Down My Barns,* wrote, "it is equally difficult to preserve one's soul from despair in hard times, as to prevent it from becoming arrogant in prosperous circumstances".[59] The Fool's sin, he says, was to "consider not how to distribute to others according to their needs, but rather how, after having received so many good things, you might rob others of the benefit".[60] He goes on vividly (and maybe a bit strangely to our urban ears), "Wells become more productive if they are drained completely, while they silt up if they are left standing. Thus wealth left idle is of no use to anyone, but put to use and exchanged it becomes fruitful and beneficial for the public good".[61] The storehouses Basil concludes should be in the stomachs of the poor!

Jesus shows the folly of accruing more than you yourself need. He advocates the ethics of enough is enough. Our lives do not consist of the abundance of possessions but in being rich towards God. Equally we have no idea of our years on earth; we are to be generous to others and to God. In this way we will avoid the tragedy of being like the Rich Fool.

## Parable of the Shrewd or "Unjust" Steward and the Parables of the Pounds or Minas (Luke 16:1–13; 19:11–27)

The remaining two parables in Luke's Gospel that teach about the use of money without a particular focus on the poor are the Parables of the Minas or Pounds and the parable of the Shrewd Steward. Both teach a commendable use of money, but both have strong contexts to explore. Furthermore Luke places this parable immediately after the story of Zacchaeus (19:1–10) which shows the effect of salvation on the use of money.

The Parable of the Minas (19:11–27) is a variation of the parable of the Talents (Matthew 21:33–46). There is general agreement that the framework of the parable is composed by Luke, but it is also thought, by Jeremias[62], that the parable was based on another source—maybe a collection of parables which was suggested in the Introduction. There are variations between Matthew and Luke: in Matthew's account, variable amounts of money are given to the servants; in Matthew there are three servants, in Luke ten; and in Matthew, the context is of a nobleman entrusting money to his servants whilst going on a long journey, while in Luke it is based around the precedent of a nobleman going to a far country to receive a kingdom.

The context of the parable in Luke gives a particular theological twist. The idea of a nobleman going on a journey to a far country to receive a kingdom was familiar to the Jews of Jesus' day. Most recently, Archelaus, the son of Herod the Great, went to Rome to petition the Emperor that he might succeed to his father's kingdom. In fact he was given only half of the kingdom, but the idea of a Jewish ruler petitioning Rome for their rule was familiar: Herod the Great, Antipas, and Agrippa I had done the same.[63] The parable is probably analogous to Jesus leaving the disciples and entrusting them with gifts for use by them, while he not only receives the Kingdom from the hand of his Father but also then waits to return while his servants use what he has given to them.

The servants are given a comparatively small sum of money, ten minas (about three months wages), to care for to use and invest until their master returns. They are ungrateful to their master, indeed they "hate him", saying, "We do not want him to rule over us" (19:14). But the master, having received his kingdom, calls the ten to account. Only three of them report: one has made ten more, another five more minas—both earning a "Well done, good servant!" and the reward of ruling over a corresponding number of cities in the kingdom (19:15–19); contrastingly one did nothing, wrapping it in a cloth and waiting.

The rest of the parable focuses on the fate of the man who had done nothing. His attitude towards his master was one of fear, it seems, paralysing him into inaction. He feared making a loss so he risked nothing and consequently has nothing to show for his master's investment. He is condemned; what was originally given to him was distributed to the other faithful servants, "for to everyone who has, more will be given, but from the one has not, even what he has will be taken away" (19:26), and he is cut down. Although the severity of the punishment is shocking to us it was in keeping with what happened in those days.[64]

What may be deduced from this parable, with regard to the use of money or talents, is that we hold both on loan. We must give an account of our use of them in this life. As we see from elsewhere, this must surely include our use of what we have for relieving the needs others, especially the poor and vulnerable. Good use will be rewarded with more responsibility, bad use will be judged for what it is. Nor is God unable to reward further those who have been bold and faithful with giving them even more. He is not aiming for equality but for productivity. The objection of the crowd to those with much receiving yet more, even at the expense of the one who has little, was that was exactly what he intended: "To everyone who has more will be given, but from the one who has not, even what he has will be taken away" (19:26). Such a salty kind of conclusion is not only bracing but it finds a seaworthy comparison in its companion parable of the Shrewd Steward.

The parable of the Unjust (itself a moral conclusion on the parable—was he unjust?) Steward or Shrewd (maybe a better adjective) Manager is our last parable unique to Luke about the use of money. The parable is in Luke 16, a chapter almost entirely devoted to teaching about money, concluding as it does, after strictures about the Pharisees' love of money, with the parable of the Rich Man and Lazarus, which we have already looked at. There is no particular context to the telling of this parable, Luke simply says: "Jesus told his disciples: 'there was a rich man whose manager was

accused of wasting his possessions'" (16:1). Although the manager had a
poor track record in looking after his master's assets (16:2) for which he
was sacked, when it came to using money to make friends he knew what
to do. He was shrewd. Dishonest in the past, his final action as manager
is commended by his master or Jesus for its shrewdness (16:8).

His shrewdness consisted *not* in dishonestly reducing the debts owed
to his master but rather in discounting all accrued interest charges on
the debts, which should not have been charged anyhow under Jewish
usury laws.[65] The high rates of interest were not unknown, and if the story
had a provenance from Egypt it was in line with interest charges there.
Derrett has produced evidence to demonstrate that Jewish and Greek
readers would understand the original bill to contain an interest charge
and also that in Egypt the then rate of interest on comestibles (e.g. oil,
wheat, and pulses) was fixed at 50 per cent.[66] Not a payday loan charge,
but nevertheless a high interest charge.

At the end of the parable Jesus draws out a number of points. Though
dishonest in the past, the manager is commended in this instance for his
shrewdness. He has done what children of the light fail to do, that is make
money work for them, in this case "to gain friends". Giving money away
not only gains friends but is also a sign of salvation. Generosity should
be a sign of grace, and grace is the means of entry into heaven (see 16:9:
"I tell you, use worldly wealth to gain friends for yourselves, so that when
it is gone, you will be welcomed into eternal dwellings"). Furthermore,
Jesus once again appeals for trustworthiness over wealth. The person who
is trustworthy over what is not theirs is more likely to be given property
of his or her own (16:12).

The parables are pre-eminently about the right use of wealth: it is to
help us look after the poor rather than isolate us from them; it is to be
used productively in whatever amounts; it is not to be stock-piled for our
own entertainment but the storehouses of our wealth should be in the
lives of others; and lastly we are to use wealth shrewdly making the most
from its power. Yes, it is powerful and can dominate, but if we are freed
from its power by service to God then it brings an exuberant freedom and
joy. The final lesson given by Jesus in Luke 16, that we cannot serve God
and money, is further illustrated by two encounters with people who had
money at the centre of their lives, the Rich Young Ruler and Zacchaeus.

It is time to learn from these two contrasting encounters. In Luke they are back-to-back stories.

## The Rich Young Ruler and Zacchaeus (Luke 18:18–30 and 19:1–10)

The Rich Young Ruler and Zacchaeus could not have been more different characters. Zacchaeus worked for the Roman authorities gathering taxes for them. Since he was the chief tax collector for Jericho, a not insignificant town, it must have been a lucrative post. He was given, in effect, a tax farm, whereby he was supposed to turn over set amounts at the end of the year to the Romans, but anything he collected over and above that he could keep.[67] He was unpopular for collaborating with the Romans but maybe more so for extracting money beyond what was due to him or the Romans. For his collaboration and for his extortionate tax gathering he was hated (see 19:7–8).

The Rich Young Ruler was quite different. Included in both Matthew (19:16–30) and Mark (10:17–30), the story depicts an earnest young man of wealthy background genuinely seeking salvation or eternal life but who finds the challenge of selling everything and giving it to the poor too much to undertake. In Mark we are told that Jesus "loved him" (10:21), and in each of three Gospels we are told that it is easier for a camel to pass through the eye of a needle than a rich man enter the Kingdom of Heaven (Luke 18:25, Matthew 19:24, and Mark 10:25). Only such things, which are humanly impossible, are made possible by God (Matthew 19:26; Mark 10:27; Luke 18:27). Or, to put it another way, only extraordinary grace can make it possible for a young man to part from his inheritance and give it all away to the poor: St Francis achieved it, Ignatius Loyola did also, and, in a different tradition, C.T. Studd in the 1880s gave up a fortune of £29,000 to serve God in China, India, and Africa. But this young ruler could not *yet* do it.

But there is an irony in these two stories being juxtaposed uniquely in Luke's Gospel. The respected, religious, and pious rich young ruler could not do what the rapacious, corrupt, and irreligious chief tax collector could do. Called down by name by Jesus from his hide-out in the sycamore tree, Zacchaeus hosted Jesus for a meal in his house. He "welcomed him gladly" and with salvation coming to his house declared: "here and now I give half my possessions to the poor, and If I have cheated anybody out of anything, I will pay back four times" (19:8). On those terms he may not have given away his *entire* fortune, but it must have been approaching it. What the rich young ruler could not do, he did: the experience of forgiveness and acceptance by Jesus in Zacchaeus' life was enough to take him like a camel through the eye of the needle, whereas the more dutiful approach of the young ruler got him stuck half way. He was willing, but did not have the motivation of grace to get him all the way through!

Luke makes a vivid point when it comes to generous giving to the poor; religious duty is not enough to loosen the purse strings in an act of extraordinary and sacrificial giving; hilarious, spontaneous giving is the result of a super-abundance of God's grace. Whereas Zacchaeus gave out of his unexpected joy, the rich young ruler could not give out of his dutiful observance of the Law (18:23a). He need a further touch of grace; maybe that came later!

## Taxes (Luke 20:19–26)

"In this world nothing can be certain except death and taxes", wrote Benjamin Franklin and no doubt Jesus would have agreed—perhaps adding the rider that death need not be the end. There were two common taxes in Jesus' day, those owing to the Romans and those owing to the Temple; this latter Tax although levied by the Temple was more dubious. Jesus gave advice about both. When asked about paying taxes to Rome and whether it was lawful (Luke 20:20ff), he requested a denarius coin. He then asked whose inscription was on it and then famously said, "Give to Caesar what is Caesar's and to God what is God's". In this way he avoided the trap that had been set for him by his questioners and the pitfalls inherent in the question: the pitfall of an answer that did not oblige the Jews to pay the Romans taxes—hence repudiating their rule and making Jesus vulnerable to the charge of insurgency, and the pitfall of not rendering to God what was his. Jesus simply said, do both!

His response to the Temple Tax, which is set out in an incident in Matthew's Gospel, shows Jesus only indirectly paying this tax (Matthew 17:24–27). It seems that he regards himself and all true sons of Israel as exempt from it and he meets its demand by the miraculous catch of a fish with a coin its mouth! A useful way of paying taxes! But what he does commend is the free gift of the widow's offering to the Temple treasury (21:1–4). Proportionately, her generosity was greater than the gifts of all the rich people.

## The Test

For Luke money was a test. Our handling of it is a test of our salvation. If our treasure is truly in heaven then we will *not* make it our aim to fill bank vaults on earth. Our storehouses will be in the hearts of the poor. If our hearts have been truly embraced by the lavish grace of God, they, in turn, will not baulk at acts of extraordinary generosity, and maybe for some this will mean giving everything away. In his anthology of Jesus' teaching about money, Luke suggests that our attitude to money is a mixture of responsibility and freedom: freedom to live lightly to it and be generous with it, but also responsible in our use of the wealth and gifts we have, and so advancing the Kingdom and blessing the poor.

# CHAPTER 7

# The Spirit and the Kingdom

So far we have seen that the tilt of this Gospel is clearly towards the outsider. Outsiders were present at Jesus' birth. The mandate for his ministry, as expressed at Nazareth, was for the outsider. At the centre of many of the parables was the figure of the outsider: lost, rebellious, or ostracised. Of the two sexes, women in the Gospel responded with a spirituality, which was often more mature and perceptive of what Jesus had come to do and who he really was than their male counterparts. The Apostles, who were the closest disciples to Jesus, even in the last hours, were concerned about their own status in the Kingdom (22:24, and earlier 9:46ff). In Luke's Gospel there is a marked concern for the poor, who by definition were outsiders. And the test in the Gospel of whether salvation had reached someone's heart was whether it had reached their pockets: to give to the poor, unlike Dives who kept it all to himself, was truly a mark of the Gospel reaching the core of someone's being. Zacchaeus did what the rich young ruler could not yet do. And the overarching setting for all this activity was, and is, the Kingdom that Jesus preached. And the overwhelming power, which enabled the manifestation of this Kingdom, was the Spirit. Jesus proclaimed the Kingdom; and the Spirit demonstrated it in the lives of people, as well as in the environment, what that Kingdom looked like.

There has been a marked tendency in the past to neglect the reality of the Kingdom in our formulation of creedal statements, whether it is the Nicene or Apostles Creed, or a formulation of belief by an evangelical organisation. There is much on the beginning and end of Jesus' life, his conception and nativity, and even more on the efficacy of his death and resurrection, but very little of what he did in the middle.[68] It is as if that central section of his ministry was less significant, or was incidental—but of course they belong together. "The Gospels are telling us that the whole story belongs together: the Kingdom and the Cross are part of one another" and the main theme of the Gospels is that "in and through Jesus the Messiah, Israel's God reclaims his sovereign rule over Israel and the World".[69] If the wider picture was this re-establishing of God's kingship in the world, the more focused outcome of Jesus' presence in Palestine was the making known of the reality of the Kingdom in the lives of ordinary people. He restored hope and dignity to their lives. St Matthew tells us that when Jesus saw the crowds "He had compassion on them because they were harassed and helpless, like sheep without a shepherd" (Matthew 9:36). Naturally, his response was to preach the good news of the Kingdom and heal every disease and sickness, transforming the lives of the people and giving hope. This was the coming rule of the King.

In Peter Shaffer's play *Amadeus*, the court composer Salieri contrasts his operas with those of Mozart. Salieri's are ponderous, unexciting and conventional: taking well-known legends from the classics or folklore and turning them into worthy but plodding musical arrangements. Salieri complains that, by contrast, Mozart has taken ordinary people—barbers and chambermaids—and he has made them gods and heroes; whereas Salieri took gods and heroes and made them ordinary.[70] Likewise, Jesus took ordinary people like tax collectors, fishermen, and prostitutes and made them leaders of a new community in the Kingdom of God. So what did Jesus do, according to Luke?

## What Did Jesus Do?

There was no mistaking what Jesus had come to do. In Luke chapter 4, we have already seen how Jesus took the opportunity at the beginning of his ministry to announce what he had come to do and how, having been thrown out of Nazareth (Luke 4:29–30), he started to fulfil this ministry at Capernaum. Using Isaiah (61:1–2), Jesus had said that he was anointed (by the Spirit) to preach good news to the poor, proclaim freedom to the captives, recovery of sight to the blind, to release the oppressed and proclaim the year of the Lord's favour (4:18–19). On one Sabbath in Capernaum (Luke 4:31ff and Mark 1:21–39) he demonstrated what this meant in practice: delivering a man from an evil spirit in the synagogue, curing Simon Peter's mother in law who was sick from a fever, and then healing many who were brought to his door at sunset. These were rays of the Kingdom of God brought by his presence and power to the lakeside communities where he was ministering. On being found by the agitated disciples (Mark 1:36–37) and the local townspeople (Luke 4:42) the morning after these events, they pressed him to stay but Jesus replied, "I *must* preach the good news of the Kingdom of God to other towns also, because that is why I was sent" (4:43). This is an important statement that is worth looking at in detail.

Sometimes, Christians have given the impression that the preaching and demonstrating of the Kingdom was the *hors d'oeuvre* before the main course of Jesus' ministry—namely his passion, crucifixion and resurrection—and that in some way the words and actions of Jesus in his ministry were just a preliminary to what he had *really* come to do, which was his sacrificial death and resurrection. But there is no need to separate what God has joined together seamlessly. The making known in real ways of the nature of the Kingdom in Jesus' ministry was the essential prelude to the great redemptive and empowering events of Jesus' passion and resurrection which then made that Kingdom open to all believers. Without the Cross, by which God deals with our sins and reconciles himself to our predicament, we could never be able to enter a Kingdom of his presence and goodness from which we were formerly excluded by our failures. Equally, without the Resurrection there is no hope of eternal life for us, no redemption of our bodies, no possibility of joining an existence which is heralded by Jesus' own resurrection, and no promise of a new world order which will swallow up all that is marred and fallen in the present one. The events of the Crucifixion and Resurrection make possible the fulfilment of the Kingdom, our entrance into that kingdom and its final triumph.

Now Jesus himself made this plain when pressed to stay in Capernaum by both his disciples and the townspeople that he "must" do something for which purpose he was sent. It is worth looking at this sentence in detail. What is it that he must do? He must preach the kingdom of God. How will he do that?

After a very full day's ministry in Capernaum, Jesus sought privacy early in the morning to pray to his Father. But the town's people had other ideas, they wanted more of his healing and teaching. They gathered round his door and finding that he was not there, questioned his disciples as to his whereabouts. Somewhat frustrated, the disciples reproached Jesus with the words: "everyone is looking for you!" (Mark 1:37). But in response, in Luke's account which follows Marks closely, Jesus says, "I *must* preach the good news of the Kingdom to the other towns also, because that it why I was sent" (4:43). The Greek is emphatic: he must do this.[71] The sense of the additional clause is even more compelling: for this reason Jesus was sent. There are two important words in the original Greek worth exploring. Firstly *euaggelisasthai* and *apestalen:* the former word means to announce the good news (we would say to evangelise) and the latter word means to be sent (to be an apostle, i.e. one who is sent). Jesus says he is under a divine commission, or a pre-eminent obligation to announce the Kingdom, just as, in the same way, he was under a divine commission (of his own voluntary making) to suffer for the redemption of humankind (see Luke 9:22, 13:33, 17:25, 19:5, 22:37, 24:7, and 26:44). The point is, just as the Scriptures *must* be fulfilled and the Son of Man must suffer, so too *must* Jesus announce the good news of the Kingdom for which he was sent (apostle). It was as much an obligation to preach the Kingdom as to die on the Cross and rise again: they were the two sides of the Son's mission and the Father's commission, and of course they were performed in the power of the Spirit.

Jesus makes it clear that he has come to preach and demonstrate the Kingdom: that is the reality of God's rule—what it is like and how to live in it. It is the bringing into the present of that which will come about perfectly in the future, namely with the Lordship of Christ.[72] As Eldon Ladd succinctly writes, the Kingdom is the presence of the future.[73] Through the Gospel this imperative is made clear. Luke tells us that "After this, Jesus travelled about from one town and village to another, proclaiming the good news of the Kingdom of God" (8:1), and again in meeting the crowds, "He welcomed them and spoke to them about the Kingdom of God, and healed those who need healing" (9:11). His parables taught about the Kingdom and its life (e.g. 13:18, 19:11); his miracles were signs of the presence of the Kingdom (11:20); his encounters, as with the rich young ruler, led to reflections on the Kingdom (18:24ff); his death was the means of entry into the Kingdom (23:43) and the Resurrection was the harbinger of this new Kingdom. The Kingdom was always at the centre of Jesus' worldview, the eschatological framework of his ministry and the fulfilment of God's great salvation plan. It lies at the heart of Jesus' work and being, it was also what the disciples were commissioned to make known, and to this important aspect of his work we must now turn. Twice in Luke's Gospel disciples are sent out to make known the Kingdom.

## What the Disciples were Commissioned to do (Luke 9:1–9, 10:1–24)

It is sometimes said that Jesus came not to show us what he could do, as the Son of God, so much as to show us what *we* could do as his followers. There is more than a grain of truth in this, although John makes it clear that the signs Jesus performed were primarily to enable people to believe: "Believe" Jesus says to Philip "on the evidence of the miracles themselves" (John 14:11b). Furthermore, Jesus said that his disciples would do "even greater things than these (his miracles)" (John 14:11b, 12b), that is greater not so much in the quality of the miracles performed (for what could be more powerful or perfect than Jesus' own miracles) but greater rather in the scope and frequency of their occurrence, because Jesus said the age of the Spirit would universalise his ministry which hitherto had been tethered to his own whereabouts and to his own time.

If in John's Gospel the signs are especially a demonstration of the glory and authority of Christ, they are also the precursor to what the church will do in the future in Christ's name and power. If Jesus anticipates this as we have seen in John 14, the synoptic Gospels give us a glimpse of what this will actually mean or look like in the sending out of Apostles and the Seventy-Two. The three Synoptic Gospels each record the sending out of the Apostles on what looks like an exercise in mission and evangelism, but it is Luke who alone extends this to include the sending out of the

Seventy-Two (Luke 9:1–9 and 10:1–24). They powerfully demonstrated the nature of the Kingdom and the role of the church in making it visible.

The two passages in Luke which record the sending out of the Twelve and the Seventy-Two form a model for the mission of the church, they have in them the characteristics for the mission of God through his church, his people. The mission is unchanging. It is to announce and demonstrate the Kingdom. There seem to be four principles common both to the mission of the Twelve and the Seven.

Firstly, they are to make the theme of their preaching the Kingdom of God: "preach the kingdom of God and heal the sick" (Luke 9:2) or "Heal the sick who are there and tell them, 'The kingdom of God has come near you'" (10:9). The preaching, it seems, is not only in word but also in deed. The fact that the preaching of the Kingdom is closely associated with the healing of the sick or the freeing of the demonised means that it was always envisaged that preaching—the act of announcing the good news—was not without its witness of God acting in power to make real and present this kingdom.

As I write it is the end of August, and during this month I have heard of preaching and healing around Britain and overseas. At one of our Summer Conventions, New Wine, I have heard of people receiving their sight, others having deafness healed, and one woman in a congregation known to me having her sight restored. And the Kingdom of God was preached to thousands with many coming to faith for the first time. Equally, one of our children went for some weeks to Iris Ministries in Mozambique. There, outreach teams went out to the rural areas and a care team was set up to take out worms from the feet of children, and the good news was made known by means of the Jesus Film based on this Gospel. Care was given and the Kingdom was made known in word and deed, many responded. So the first ingredient of the mission of the twelve and 72 was the making known of the Kingdom.

Secondly, the disciples were lightly equipped for their task. They took very little with them. Jesus says to the Seventy-Two that they will be vulnerable, "Go! I am sending you out like lambs amongst wolves. Do not take a purse, or a bag or sandals; and do not greet anyone on the road" (10:3). In other words, they were to be lightly equipped, and entirely dependent on the provision of God for them. If there is a sense of missionary training in this command (which would be appropriate to someone learning to be dependent on God in what seems like a short-term mission), there are still principles for the longer-term mission of the church. The church has too easily taken up positions of power or status in its mission, its leaders in the historic churches too prone to enjoy trappings of secular power and authority. The Franciscan movement in the thirteenth century was a conscious departure from all such too human tendencies. The disciples were to go lightly.

They were also to be committed to the places to which they went and were warmly received. "Whatever house you enter, stay there until you leave the town" (9: 4). And "When you enter a house, first say, 'Peace to this house'. If a man of peace is there, your peace will rest upon him; if not it will return to you. Stay in the house, eating and drinking whatever they give you, for the worker deserves his wages. Do not move around from house to house" (10:5–7). In other words, they were to be committed to those who respond openly, warmly, and positively to their presence and message. They were to be content and recognise that this was God's provision. The man of peace was one pre-disposed to respond to the message of the Kingdom.

Lastly, if they receive a hostile reception from a whole community then they were to make a symbolic act "indicative of the lack of fellowship" (Marshall, p. 351), they shook the dust from their feet and moved on. The inference appears to be that time is short, the days are urgent, and if some will not hear, others will; and people's response is down to them, they are responsible for what they do with the message (10:10–12).

These then are the main principles of the mission that Jesus sent his followers on, both the Twelve and the Seventy-Two. They may have been meant for a particular time and place, but they contain principles, which are for all time. We are always to make the Kingdom central to our preaching and action, we are to travel lightly, we are to stay where we receive a welcome until the work of announcing and teaching the Kingdom is done, and we are to recognise that some will refuse both us and our message. And what results followed! Jesus said he saw "Satan fall like lightning from heaven" (10:18). The mission of God dethroned Satan from his seat. Jesus acknowledged the authority he had given his disciples. Their mission filled Jesus with joy (10:21), and it was the means whereby the Father revealed the Son and Son revealed the Father (10:22). Indeed kings and prophets had wanted to see these things, but now they were common currency. The Kingdom was made known to the outsider and the disciples were commissioned to do this, and soon it was to be done in the power of the Spirit.

## The Spirit and the Kingdom

Two Gospels, John and Luke, especially emphasise the work of the Spirit. John's pneumatology (his description of the Spirit's work) is quite extensive. The Spirit brings a person to new birth (3:5–6). The Spirit will well up in someone like a spring of water gushing out in life-giving power from within a person (7:37ff), if only he or she will come to Jesus and drink, and this will happen to all once Jesus has opened the Kingdom of Heaven to all believers following his death (7:39b). The Spirit is promised to the new community of disciples once Jesus has returned to the Father (14:15ff). He will ask the Father and the Father will give the Spirit to the church, his flock. The Spirit is variously described in John's Gospel as the Comforter, Counsellor, Paraclete, or Advocate. John frequently describes what the Spirit will do both for the disciple—assuring, guiding, and helping her—and also what he will do in the (unbelieving) world, convicting the world of truth (truth about themselves and truth about God 16:8ff). The gift of the Spirit will cement the relationship of love and trust between the disciple and their Lord (14:20), and will also guide the believer into all truth, reminding the Apostles of all that Jesus taught (16:12ff), and subsequently teaching the church the significance of Jesus teaching (16:14–15).

In summary, John especially teaches us about the relationship of the Spirit to the other persons of the Trinity. He shows that the Spirit will indwell the disciple bringing him into the Kingdom, assuring him and guiding him in all aspects of the truth. And outside the church, the Spirit is at work in the world to convince those not yet Christians of what is

true. And much of this teaching is only found in John, although Paul
later develops it.

By contrast, Luke gives us a different perspective to the work of the
Spirit. Luke gives little away about the relationship of the Spirit to the
Father and Son *jointly*, at least not in an "ontological sense", that is strictly
in terms of their co-existence or how they relate together or their mode
of being. But passages of scripture surrounding the birth of Jesus and
John the Baptist are bursting with the activity of the Spirit (see 1:15, 1:35,
1:41, 1:67, 2:27). More especially, Luke does describe the activity of the
Spirit in relation to prayer and the promulgation of the Kingdom. Since
Luke makes clear that the priority of Jesus' ministry is the establishing
of the Kingdom, both in his ministry as well as through his death and
resurrection and returning to the Father, he also demonstrates that it is the
through the work of the Spirit in him that Jesus proclaims the arrival of
the Kingdom both through word (his preaching) and deed (his miracles).

As Graham Tomlin writes, "The kingdom of God is what happens
when the Spirit comes".[74] God is experienced. Food is multiplied to feed
the hungry and poor. The sick are healed. The outsider is welcomed. "The
kingdom always has this sense of the presence of God in power, and the
resulting transformation of the world. The kingdom is what happens
when the Spirit comes".[75] Without the Spirit in Jesus, the Kingdom would
not have come. This is made clear at the Baptism of Jesus when the Spirit
equipped Jesus for the work that lay ahead (3:22, 4:1ff). Furthermore in
his sermon in the Synagogue at Nazareth, which began with the quotation
from Isaiah that, "the Spirit of the Lord is on me because he has anointed
me", Jesus makes clear that his own activity is inspired by the Spirit and
this was the fulfilment of his Father's plan. So when John the Baptist's
disciples ask for signs that Jesus is truly the Messiah, Jesus tells them to
tell John what they have seen and heard: "the blind receive their sight,
the lame walk, those who have leprosy are cured, the deaf hear, the dead
are raised, and the good news is preached to the poor" (7:21ff). And a
little later he says "if I drive out demons by the finger of God (a metaphor
perhaps for the Spirit) then the Kingdom of God has come to you" (11:20).
In short: Jesus came to make real the Kingdom. The Kingdom is where
God has his way. Only the Son empowered by the Spirit can manifest the

Kingdom of God. And in the Kingdom all people find their true home; the outsider is no longer estranged.

The Spirit in Luke's writings is the member of the Godhead who, with and through Jesus following his Baptism, activates, first through Jesus and then through his church, the presence of the Kingdom contemporaneously. The church or the community of believers first birthed in the events of Pentecost, as recorded only by Luke in the Acts of the Apostle, now points to the reality of the Kingdom bringing that reality to bear, wherever the church is found. The church is not the Kingdom, but is at its best a signpost to the Kingdom. The Spirit enables the church to fulfil its mandate, a continuance of that mandate first given by Isaiah and then used by Jesus in Luke 4 as the foundation of his ministry. As one of the early Fathers, Basil of Cappadocia, wrote in the first treatise on the Holy Spirit in the early centuries of the church, "He is present as whole to each and wholly present everywhere. He is portioned out impassibly and participated in as a whole. He is like a sunbeam whose grace is present to the one who enjoys him as if he were present to each one who is fit to receive, as if he were present to him alone, and still he sends out his grace that is complete and sufficient for all".[76] Supremely therefore, the Spirit is the one who indwells each of Christ's followers but works in the world to bring the outsider into the grace of God. This is clear through the ministry of Jesus in the Gospel fulfilling the words he spoke in the Synagogue of Nazareth. It is what the Spirit continued to do, as Luke recorded in the Acts of the Apostle, but possibly it is supremely what the Spirit does in the events of the Passion, the Crucifixion and the Resurrection. To this we must now turn.

CHAPTER 8

# Outsiders at the Passion, Crucifixion, and Resurrection

For a moment let's consider what it means to be an insider or an outsider. Hitherto we have seen the outsider mostly in terms of being someone who is on the edge of Jewish society in New Testament times for moral, ethnic, social, or sexual reasons; but there are other ways of being an outsider. It can also be used simply in relation to whether someone is on the inside or the outside of a group. A gang member will be an insider; indeed they may well find their security, identity, and meaning by being part of a gang. Equally we often define ourselves by belonging to a particular group, which gives us identity. It might be a political group aligning us, in the UK, with the Conservative, Labour or Liberal Democrat parties. If we belong to one of these parties it defines our aspirations, values, and associations politically. Or again, belonging to interest groups or sports-clubs will further define us as people whether it is rowing, archery, football, cricket, or rugby. Clubs of all kinds express our interests, talents, and disposition. We either belong or do not belong: we are on the fringe or beyond the fringe; we are either getting deeper into a group or our ties are weakening. The church should be the one human group in which the outsider should quickly feel at home and accepted, but sadly that is always not the case.

The final events of Jesus' life: his trial, crucifixion, and resurrection had an extraordinary power to test all groupings and to define loyalties freshly, and sometimes unexpectedly. These events revealed to people where their political, religious, spiritual, and personal loyalties or weaknesses were.

The events of Christ's passion revealed weakness and courage, cowardice and bravery, faith and fear in an exceptional way. And in some cases loyalties so changed during the course of these events that a person ended up in quite a different place from the one in which they had begun. So we shall see that Peter begins as a powerful insider in the band of Jesus' disciples but then leaves through fear and denial, going outside to weep, but re-gains his place later through re-affirmation of his love for Jesus and forgiveness. Judas by contrast leaves the disciples of Jesus, never to return. Pilate veers from one direction to another, eventually deciding to remain on the side of Imperial Rome rather than on the side of the Kingdom about which he had heard. A seemingly random outsider, Simon of Cyrene, found himself carrying the Cross of Jesus. And while Jesus is being crucified, one criminal crucified alongside him moved from despair to hope, as Jesus promised him paradise in response to his faith. And most surprisingly of all, Jesus himself, so changed on account of his Resurrection, becomes an outsider to the very people whom he had previously led and formed. It as if everyone moved around during these life-changing hours so that in the end the insiders become outsiders and outsiders becomes insiders. It is as if all previous allegiances are thrown up in the air by these momentous and world changing events, and they come down in different and more tested forms, compared with before. We will trace each of these stories through the passion narratives of St Luke and show Luke's own special heart for the outsider, which in turn reflects that of his Lord.

## Judas Iscariot (Luke 22: 1–6)

Judas Iscariot moved from being part of one group, the disciples of Jesus, to being a complete outsider placing himself beyond, it seems, the grace of God. His was a tragic movement. It is John who tells us that he was the treasurer for the disciples, but this presented him with temptations that he could not overcome. Objecting to the use of Mary's expensive perfume for the use of anointing Jesus before his passion, we are told by John, "he

[Judas] did not say this because he cared about the poor but because he was a thief; as keeper of the money bag, he used to help himself to what was put into it" (John 12:6). It seems that a creeping love of money got the better of him: corrupting his spiritual and moral integrity and luring him into his most heinous betrayal. In Luke's account we are told that Satan entered Judas at the beginning of the Feast of the Unleavened Bread (22:1), while John tells us that this occurred during the Last Supper when Jesus gave him the piece of bread dipped in herbs (which was normally a particular honour; John 13:27ff). It was then that Satan entered him according to John and he left the group of disciples in the Upper Room and, we are told, "it was night" (John 13:30b). Whenever the precise occasion occurred in which Judas was in some way overwhelmed by Satan, he had already laid himself open to such an assault by his greed for money. He had agreed to betray Jesus for thirty pieces of silver. His love for money overcame all his previous spiritual aspirations and cast him headlong into this act of betrayal. Yet when he had the money it turned to ashes in his pocket.

Just as Judas had taken the silver from the Chief Priests and the Temple Guard all too readily and then betrayed Jesus in the Garden of Gethsemane, so, following Jesus' condemnation to death, Judas swiftly fell into deep remorse. Judas knew he had sinned, for as he says "he had betrayed innocent blood" (Matthew 27:4). But, unlike with repentance, there appeared to be no way back to the grace of God from this remorse. Jesus is reported to have said, "Woe to that man who betrays the Son of Man! It would be better for him if he had not been born (Matthew 26:24). Throwing the money onto the Temple floor as an act of contrition, he went and hanged himself (Matthew 27:5). If it is Matthew who gives us most of the inside story about Judas' feelings and end, whilst John gives us plenty of symbolism associated with his actions, Luke simply gives us the bare facts. For the sake of money Judas betrayed his Master, money as so often in Luke's gospel shows a person's true spiritual state. For money Judas was content to betray his Lord. Its power drew him from being inside the group of disciples to being outside of the Kingdom and the community which he had joined and been chosen for. The purse strings unravelled his discipleship; it need not have, but in his case, given his weakness, it did. Another disciple faced an almost as acute crisis as Judas, but he was able to return. Having been outside he was able to come back in, and he was of course Simon Peter.

## Simon Peter (Luke 22:31- 38, 54–62)

Simon Peter was the leading Apostle. He had recognised and confessed Jesus to be the Messiah. (Luke 9: 18ff). We know from the record of the Gospels that he was headstrong, sometimes rash, presumptuous, and forthright; often he had to go backwards before going forward again. The French have a phrase for it: *reculer pour mieux sauter*, to go back in order to move forward again—like a high jumper attempting a jump. But Peter's worst setback, from which he did eventually recover through the grace of Jesus, was his threefold denial of Christ which caused him both his greatest grief and his deepest spiritual lesson. It is a two-part story. The Synoptic Gospel writers tell the first part, the sequel is found in John (John 21). It is a well known story, yet it shows how an individual who was more at the centre of things than most, who found himself outside in the cold *literally*, but then is later restored to a central role in the movement to which he first belonged. Luke gives a vivid and telling record of this story.

During the Last Supper, Jesus warned Peter of his impending spiritual trial, "Simon, Simon," he said, using his original birth-name, possibly to impress on him the seriousness of what awaited him, "Satan has asked to sift you as wheat (see Job 1:6ff) but I have prayed for you, Simon, that your faith may not fail. And when you have turned back strengthen your brothers" (Luke 22:31–32). Jesus quite clearly knew the test that awaited Peter and the temptation to despair for him, but Jesus prayed that he would recover and be able to strengthen his brothers. Peter was having none of this and replied with ignorance and brashness, "Lord" he said "I am ready to go with you to prison and to death" (22:33). But Jesus, as we know, predicted that Peter would deny him three times before the cock crowed. Having slept when Jesus was in agony in the garden of Gethsemane, they were unprepared for what lay ahead and had not followed the Lord's advice of praying that they might not enter temptation (22:40).

After the arrest of Jesus in Gethsemane at the instigation of Judas, Peter finds himself following the Temple guard and their prisoner, Jesus, into the High Priests' compound. There he waits, warming himself by the fire, which they make in the courtyard. Three times Peter is challenged that he is one of Jesus' disciples by a servant girl and two others. The bravado has gone, the confidence has evaporated, and without stopping to think—driven by a bewildered fear—Peter denies Jesus three times and then the cock crows. And suddenly Peter realises what he has done. At that very moment when he froze in the shame at what had transpired, Luke tells us that Jesus "turned and looked straight at Peter" (22: 61). It was most probably the most devastating moment of Peter's life. He went outside and wept bitterly. He was now the outsider, but Jesus had prayed for him that he would "turn back and strengthen his brothers."

Peter was restored. He came back from the bitterness of being out in the cold on the night of Jesus' crucifixion to being at the centre of the new Community centred around the resurrection of Jesus and the Followers of the Way, as Christians were first known. The restoration of Simon Peter occurred on the shore of Galilee after a further miraculous catch of fish, a repeat of the miracle that had happened at Peter's original call (see Luke 5:1ff). Three times Peter affirmed that he loved Jesus, and three times he was told to feed the flock of God (John 21:15–17). Peter was re-commissioned as the leading Apostle; he was now in a position to lead the church into its future as he did on the day of Pentecost. Peter is the perpetual example of a person being restored after a failure. He went from being an insider to being an outsider, to being restored to his central role and calling. Our next person from the gallery of characters that surround Jesus in his final hours is Pilate. Although he knew the innocence of Jesus and the integrity of his life, he chose in the end to do what was expedient and so remained outside the Kingdom of which they spoke.

## Pontius Pilate (Luke 22:66–23:25)

The account of Jesus' trial by Pilate in Luke is more peremptory than John's account, but, nonetheless, the same ambivalence towards Jesus is obvious in Luke's account.[77] In a fuller account of their conversation in John, both kingship and truth are the subjects of their exchanges (John 18:28ff). In John it looks less like a trial and more like an advanced theology or philosophy seminar with a consummate teacher, but the stakes are far higher! Luke gives us the bare bones of Pilate's response to the prisoner, handed over to him at dawn by the High Priests anxious to see Jesus convicted and executed that day. But Pilate, having spent a short time with the prisoner, says to his accusers, "I find no basis for a charge against this man" (23:4) and again after sending him to Herod—since Jesus is a Galilean—who likewise does not sentence him, Pilate again says, "I have examined him in your presence and found no basis for your charges against him" (23:14b). In other words, Pilate saw that no proper charge deserving punishment, let alone death, could be brought against Jesus. In that case he should release him. But intimidated by the Jewish leaders' vehemence and the whipped-up animosity of the crowd, and with the cry or taunt that Pilate would be no friend of Caesar should he release Jesus, because Jesus claimed to be a king, he gave in famously washed his hands of any complicity or guilt, and handed Jesus over to his soldiers to be crucified.

Pilate had come close to acting on truth as he found it in his conversation with Jesus, but in the end he had acted guided by political instinct and expediency, sacrificing truth to intimidation and integrity to wider considerations of his career, keeping in with the Jews rather pursuing what he knew in his heart and conscience to be right. He came close to becoming part of the Kingdom of which he had heard from the lips of the King, of becoming an insider in that Kingdom rather than one wedded to the exercise of imperial power and the realpolitik of colonial administration. He saw the truth, felt the truth, but remained outside the compelling spiritual logic of the truth. He could not sacrifice what he had acquired for what he knew to be right. But another unknown man was suddenly press-ganged into the consequences of Pilate's decision and found himself to be forever changed.

## Simon of Cyrene (Luke 23:26)

Cyrene is a beautiful, verdant part of North Africa, present day Libya, where wheat, figs, vines, olives, and oranges grow, gardens flourish, and a prosperous Roman colony existed with, as almost always, a Jewish community which formed part of the Diaspora. Cyrenian Jews were commonly found in Jerusalem. Often well off themselves, these Cyrenians travelled well and some were there on the day of Pentecost (Acts 2:10), had their own Synagogue in Jerusalem called the Synagogue of the Freedmen (presumably some were ex-slaves) whose orthodox members had vehemently opposed Stephen (see Acts 6:9). One of their fellow countrymen was there in Jerusalem for the Passover with the other maybe 100,000 pilgrims that thronged the city at the Feast, throwing up encampments around the city. He too, like the leading Apostle, was called Simon. He happened to be in the "right" place at the "right" time, as Jesus struggled to carry the heavy piece of wood that formed the upright of the Cross on which he would be crucified. Weakened to the point of complete exhaustion by the soldiers' flogging, the all-night trial, and the spiritual ordeal he was about to enter, it was clear to the soldiers that he would not be able to carry this part of the cross. So the soldiers compelled a passerby to it for him. The fact that the Christian community knew Simon's name, and those of his children, Alexander and Rufus (see Mark 15:21), and his place of origin, suggests that he and they became part of the Christian community thereafter. He had been a complete stranger. His carrying of the Cross was seemingly an apparently chance arrangement, but suddenly he finds himself following Jesus to his place of execution, an event which he then presumably witnessed, and which, most probably, forever changed him. He may have carried the Cross unwillingly, forced into it by soldiers when he was simply coming in from the country, but he was never the same again. Nor was one of the criminals who was crucified with Jesus.

## The Thief on the Cross (Luke 23:32–43)

Only Luke records the conversation between Jesus and the two criminals executed either side of him. Indeed most of Luke's narrative of Jesus' actual crucifixion is take up by this conversation. Some commentators (e.g. Ellis p. 870, Howard Marshall) have therefore argued that this conversation forms the centrepiece of Luke's narrative of the Crucifixion, concentrating not so much on the event itself as the outcome of it in terms of salvation for all those, like the penitent thief, who believe.

Having forgiven the soldiers who hammered nails through his hands and feet while placing him on the cross on the ground, Jesus withstood the taunts of the religious leaders—"He saved others: let him save himself if he is the Christ of God, the Chosen One" (23:35). Above him, on the Cross itself, was the sign put there at the command of Pilate, "this is the king of the Jews" or as it is recorded in another Gospel, "Jesus of Nazareth King of the Jews" ("Iesus nazarenus rex iudaeorum", John 19:19). The soldiers too, having executed him, and gambled for his clothes, taunted him, "If you are the King of the Jews save yourself" (23:36b). For them it was part of the soldiers' harsh game of belittling their captive and gaining from his destitution, another mark of the cruel world of the Empire. But Luke reserves most space in his narrative of Jesus' crucifixion for the conversation with the two criminals, and this is surely his intended purpose: to show the effect of Jesus' death which was "a stumbling block to the Jews, folly to the Greeks" but to others "the power and the wisdom of God" (1 Corinthians 1:22ff). And it is not too fanciful to suppose that if this Gospel was being written by Luke when Paul was held prisoner in Caesarea and after accompanying Paul for much of his second missionary journey, which included his visit to Corinth, this description of the Cross was in keeping with all that Paul preached about it and which Luke must have heard repeatedly.

The conversation was, under the circumstances, both vivid and profound. One criminal joined in with the common taunts: "Aren't you the Christ? Save yourself and us!" (23:39b). The other was more perceptive, aware and above all believing. There was something about the demeanour of the prisoner next to them that gave pause for thought, reflection, and faith. This criminal was more than frank about his own wrongdoing and equally forthright about the innocence of Jesus, "We are punished justly, for we are getting what our deeds deserve. But this man has done nothing wrong" (23:41). This criminal shows knowledge of his own guilt, awareness of the innocence (sinlessness) of Jesus, and most of all, through his own spiritual perception and through some revelation that came to him, he recognised that Jesus was a King, and so famously said, "Jesus [addressing him most personally], remember me when you come into your Kingdom" (23:42). He could hardly have expected Jesus' instant and unqualified response, "I tell you the truth, today you will be with me in paradise" (23:43). If paradise is an unusual word in the New Testament, recalling the existence of creation before the Fall, the Garden of Eden, it could not have been a more contrasting and refreshing thought to someone in the throes of torture and death.[78] On the confession of faith and repentance for his own wrong, this man in an instant passed from death to life, from despair to hope, and from condemnation to liberation, and all on the word of Jesus who was dying next to him to bring just such a possibility to pass. It was the gospel in a nutshell, and the Lucan message vividly and unforgettably conveyed in a moment. No one could have been more of an outsider than this criminal to the Jewish and the Roman world alike, and no one was promised more on account of less: it was all grace and its result was joyous salvation, snatching victory from the jaws of death.

But more was to come. In a matter of days two despondent disciples were walking from Jerusalem to Emmaus pondering all that might have been and all that had happened when a third person joined them. He seemed a veritable outsider to Jerusalem and the events of the past few days, but they carefully listened to what he had to say.

## On the way to Emmaus (Luke 24:13–35)

The story of the walk to Emmaus by two disciples is one of several unique features of Luke's Gospel. Just as you could not conceive of the New Testament without the parable of the Good Samaritan or the Prodigal Son (or the Generous Father)—so integral are they to Jesus' teaching—nor could you think of the Resurrection appearances without this one of Jesus revealing himself to the two disciples in the house in Emmaus after a seven mile walk with them to the village. The story is beautifully told. It is full of irony and suspense. At the heart of the story is the fact that Jesus was not recognised, and for a time he became an outsider whilst he was at the same time the subject of the conversation. This lends a dramatic tension and a kind of delicious irony to the conversation, which is exploded at the end when Jesus is recognised.

The two disciples, one of whom is called Cleopas, were walking dejectedly to Emmaus on the day after the Sabbath, presumably having been in Jerusalem for the Festival of the Passover. They were now, it seems, returning home. Their minds must have been filled by the events of the week end, and they may have been eyewitnesses to the trial and execution of Jesus, heard the mob crying for his blood, and possibly may have seen him executed. They plaintively said, "we had hoped that he was the one who was going to redeem Israel" (24:21). Furthermore, their perplexity was only increased by the reports from the women that they had been to the tomb early, found it empty, and had seen a vision of angels. Other disciples, presumably Peter and John, had been to the tomb and found it as the women had described (see John 20:3ff).

The unknown, unrecognised stranger then began to give them a bible study from Moses through the Prophets about how the "Christ had to suffer these things and then enter his glory" (24:26–27). Later they recalled how their hearts burnt within them as they heard his teaching (24:32). It was only after they had pressed him to stay and he had gone into their house and "took bread, gave thanks, broke it, and began to give it to them" that their eyes were opened (24:31).

The nature of the story is exquisite, combining features of journey, sudden appearance, mystery, explanation from the scriptures, the echoes of the sacrament, recognition, and disappearance, which are found also in the story of the Ethiopian Eunuch (Acts 8:26ff). But here the element of hiddenness and recognition are uppermost in the account. It is as though the Resurrected Lord had become an outsider to those whom he once knew intimately. It is not that he is estranged or in any way alienated from them, but that he know dwells in a new Resurrection order of existence which is both part of and separate from our own (see also, Jesus' reply to Mary Magdalene in John 20:17). As such, this story of the walk to Emmaus is also a prequel to the Acts of the Apostles. The Resurrection marks the entrance of the Kingdom in a new way into the world, for it demonstrates both Christ's victory over death and the final victory of the rule of God over all his enemies. It is now only a matter of time before this is brought to a glorious conclusion and the Kingdom of God is made perfect, but now is the age of the Spirit and of the proclamation of the Good News by the church to the nations, until the Kingdom fully comes. In answer to the disciple's question, "are you at this time going to restore the kingdom to Israel?" Jesus replied that it was not for them to know "the times or dates the Father has set by his own authority" but they would shortly know in their own experience that they had entered the age of the Spirit and of proclamation of the Gospel, "for when the Holy Spirit comes upon you, you will be my witnesses in Jerusalem, and in all Judea and Samaria, and to the ends of the earth." (Acts 1:6–9). The Gospel was now to be preached outside the Jewish nation and Jerusalem, and Luke will show more than ever that it really is a Gospel for the outsider.

CHAPTER 9

# Jerusalem, Judea, Samaria, and the Gentiles

Any reader of the New Testament may well fail to link Luke and Acts closely together, not because they are in any doubt that they have a common author, but because the Gospel of John lies between them. The simple effect of that, for most readers, is to diminish the continuity of the two works. From the start Luke intended them to be a two-volume work with common themes but we have distanced them by placing, quite understandably, all the Gospels together.[79]

We shall probably never know the time gap between the writing of Luke's two volumes, but it may well have been short. If we are right in supposing that Luke gathered together material for his Gospel while Paul was imprisoned in Caesarea (see Acts 23:23ff), then it is quite possible that the Gospel and Acts were written soon after that research in Rome, where Luke was with Paul (2 Timothy 4:11). And this may also account for Luke's knowledge of Mark's Gospel, which was also written in Rome around AD 64. Other material common to Luke and Matthew, called Q by the scholars, was identified with Syria and quite possibly specifically with Antioch. If this is right we can say that Luke's Gospel research was done in Israel during Paul's imprisonment at Ceasarea, having accompanied Paul on his second and third missionary journey, and may well have involved time with the significant Christian community in Antioch. The Gospel and Acts could then have been written in Rome and Antioch before the destruction of Jerusalem. Such a timetable would accord well with Howard Marshall, who wrote, "the complete lack of interest in the

97

Fall of Jerusalem in Acts and the way in which that book ends its story before the death of Paul are strong indications of a date before AD 70".[80] Surely a historian of Luke's calibre, and a writer of his elegance, would have included that event, which not only fulfilled Jesus' prophecy in the Gospel (see Luke 19:41–44) but also forever changed the future of the Jews in the Classical world through the utter destruction of Jerusalem by the armies of Vespasian and Titus. So, if the Acts were written as a second volume before AD 70, the Gospel would have preceded it and have been written either in Rome or Syrian Antioch some years earlier.

The common authorship of Luke/Acts and the possibility that they were written closely together in Antioch and Rome means that common themes are likely to occur throughout Luke's corpus. The continuity is not only of authorship or of the patron, Theophilus, but also in the theological ideas, which run through the two works. Again, because the two books fall into slightly different sections of the New Testament, we tend to insulate one from the other, assuming that theological themes are not carried through from one to the other. But we can see that some of these themes, which we have already noticed in the Gospel, are present in Acts: the care of the poor (Acts 2:45, 4:32, 6:1); the use of wealth (4:34–37, 3:6), including the salutary story of Ananias and Sapphira (5:1–11); the essential priority of forgiveness of sins (2:38); the significance of prayer (1:14, 4:24ff, 6:7, 7:59–60, 9:11, 12:15); the acceptance of enemies (9:26ff); and a Gospel or Kingdom which is intended for the world.

But the supreme link, which Luke makes very clear at the outset of the Acts of the Apostles to Theophilus, is that the Gospel (Luke's "former book") demonstrates "all that Jesus *began* to do and to teach until he was taken up to heaven" (1:1–2). In other words, Luke is telling Theophilus that what Jesus *began* to do in person through his teaching and action he will *now* do through the church filled by the Spirit. It is an important interpretive key. There is no disconnect between the ministry of Jesus in person and the ministry of the church through the person of the Spirit, or at least there ought not to be. What motivated Jesus, should motivate the church; what empowered him at his Baptism should empower the church; what Jesus demonstrated to the Apostles should be enacted by the church; the Kingdom which he announced in his ministry is the same Kingdom to be pointed to by the church; the forgiveness which he procured by his passion is the forgiveness now to be proclaimed by the church. In other words, what Jesus began, he now completes through his body on earth, the church (9:5), and what he did himself he now does through his people.

Just as John states why he wrote his Gospel, that "you may believe that Jesus is the Christ, the Son of God, and that believing you may have life in his name" (see John 20:31), and Matthew's Gospel can be read in the light of the Great Commission (Matthew 28:18–20), so Luke has a single interpretative key for his theology. It is found at the end of his Gospel in the summary words of Jesus about his mission:

> This is what is written: The Christ will suffer and rise from the dead on the third day, and repentance and forgiveness of sins will be preached in his name to all nations, beginning at Jerusalem, You are witnesses of these things. I am going to send you what my Father has promised; but stay in the city until you have been clothed with power from on high.
>
> *Luke 24:46–49*

This represents the hinge of the two volumes, but not only the hinge but the key also. All that Jesus has begun to do in the Gospel was brought to its climactic conclusion by his sufferings and resurrection as the Scriptures had promised. These events now form the Gospel, which can be made real for people and communities by repentance and faith. This mission is to be executed by witnesses starting from Jerusalem, and they will be equipped by the power of the Spirit. As Bosch says, these elements of this great statement at the end of the Gospel represent "the fibres of Luke's mission theology".[81] The story of the Acts of the Apostle is the account of how the church fulfilled this commission, first the church in Jerusalem and then Gentile mission of Paul starting from Antioch.

## Prepared by Pentecost (Acts 2:1–47)

Jesus had instructed the Apostles to "stay in the city" until they had received power from on high (24:48). They waited in the Upper Room in Jerusalem for what Jesus had promised (Acts 1:4–5; John 14:16–17). After the choosing of a twelfth Apostle to replace Judas Iscariot (Acts 1:12ff), the Apostles prayed constantly, being joined by some of the woman, and in particular by Mary the mother of Jesus and his brothers (1:14). After some time the Holy Spirit came upon "all of them" (2:4) : the Spirit filled them, they were quickened by fire, they spoke in other tongues, and they were transformed. And what Jesus had promised at the end of Luke's Gospel had come about.

The purpose of the gift of the Spirit was unmistakeably clear. It was not an end in itself, but it was the creation of a missional community; it was to propel the church into mission and take this gospel to Jerusalem, Judea, and Samaria, and to the ends of the earth (Acts 1:9). We would do well to consider how the early church discharged its commission, and the answer appears to be good in parts. The temptation is to think that the Apostles fulfilled their commission perfectly, but the answer is that they were reluctant to take the gospel across those barriers which Jesus himself had crossed in his ministry, and that it took extraordinary activity by God the Holy Spirit to ensure that the barriers were traversed so that the gospel would go to Samaria, the Gentiles, and to the end of the earth. And it was the extraordinary missionary grasp of Paul that enabled the gospel to be taken to the ends of the earth.

What is absolutely clear from the day of Pentecost is that the Spirit equipped the church for mission. Just as the Spirit was active in Luke's Gospel around the birth of Jesus, as we have seen, he was now instrumental in the birth of the church. The Spirit is the one who both conceives and brings to birth; as with the Son of God (Luke 1:35) so with the church (Acts 2:17). Once again the Spirit, depicted as wind, overshadowed the Apostles and the believers, filling their lives. He gave them tongues not so much to praise him (as in 1 Corinthians 14:16) as to communicate the good news to the pilgrims in Jerusalem (Acts 2:6–11b). As they (Jews and God-fearers from the dispersion) asked what does this mean, Peter replied in a powerful and fruitful address explaining that this (what they heard and saw) was what Joel had prophesied about; and that receipt of salvation was now open to all through repentance, faith, and receiving the Spirit (2:38). Three thousand believed; suddenly the church, which began in Jerusalem and was soon scattered through the dispersion, had taken root. The day of Pentecost was a model in evangelism enacted by the Spirit. The church in Jerusalem was birthed in the teeth of opposition (like the birth of Jesus), but its spread to the other areas of Samaria and the Gentiles was not so swift, and was, in the last resort, choreographed supremely by the Spirit.

## Jerusalem Bound (Acts 3–7)

If the Gospel of Luke can be read as a journey, or progress of the Messiah, from Galilee to Jerusalem, with a pivotal point at Luke 9:51 when "Jesus resolutely set out for Jerusalem", setting his face like a flint to do so, the Acts of the Apostles can be seen as a journey (or progress of the gospel) from Jerusalem to Rome. The story begins with Peter and the Apostles in Jerusalem (Acts 1:12) and ends with Paul in Rome (Acts 28:30–31). Likewise, the story begins with Peter making known the new age of the Spirit to the pilgrims in Jerusalem who heard the message in their own tongue, and it ends with Paul "boldly and without hindrance preaching the kingdom of God" in Rome (Acts 28:31).

But the movement from Jerusalem to Rome in the Acts was not altogether smooth, nor was it undertaken without considerable persecution of the church and overruling by the Holy Spirit. The early days of the Apostles' ministry in Jerusalem could not have been headier. Jerusalem was the strategic hub of the Jewish world, the place, as Micah had promised, that "many nations would come and say, 'Come let us go up to the house of the God of Jacob. He will teach us his ways, so that we may walk in his paths'. The Law will go out from Zion, the words of the Lord from Jerusalem" (Micah 4:2). Not surprisingly it was here that the Spirit was poured on the church: the place where the Messiah had suffered and risen again on the third day as prophesied by the scriptures (Luke 24:46–49) was the place where the church was birthed. But the church and God's mission through her was not to stay there, for Jesus had said, "stay in the city until you have been clothed power from on high" (Acts 24:49b), and then again "you will receive power when the Holy Spirit comes on you; and you will be my witnesses in Jerusalem, and in Judea and Samaria and the end of the earth" (1:8). The movement of the gospel to these places, Judea, Samaria, and the ends of the earth, was not so much brought about by carefully planned missionary strategy as by the compulsion of persecution, together with the circumstantial guidance of the Spirit.

On the day of Pentecost, there was a tremendous response to Peter's address; we are told (2:41b) that three thousand believed and were baptised. By any standards of mission this was an astonishing response, as much attributable to the work of the Spirit as the event of Pentecost itself. The Jerusalem revival continued: an extraordinary healing occurred at the Gate Beautiful in the Temple area (3:1–10). Peter once again preached the message (3:11–26). The arrest of Peter and John followed, and during their appearance at the Sanhedrin they were forbidden to preach Jesus (4:17), but they went straight back to their preaching. The Apostles performed many miracles, even by their shadows falling on the sick as they lay on mats in the street. People from the surrounding towns and cities of Judea brought their sick to Jerusalem for healing (5:16). Persecution grew as the powerless of the Sanhedrin increased. The Apostles were once again arrested, but released by an Angel (5:19) who commissioned them to "God stand in the temple courts and tell the people the full message of life" (5:20). The Sanhedrin once again took council, and the famous teacher Gamaliel gave the sage advice that "If their purpose or activity is of human origin it will fail. But if it is from God, you will not be able stop these men; you will only find yourself fighting against God" (5:39). The apostles were flogged but released. But with the stoning of Stephen, one of the Seven Deacons chosen to serve at tables, persecution increased (8:2).

It was as if the very success of the church bound it to Jerusalem but its persecution scattered the Church to the areas of Judea and Samaria to which Jesus had commissioned it to go (see Acts 1:8). Luke tells us that the effect of the renewed persecution of the church that accompanied the stoning of Stephen was to scatter the believers, except the Apostles, through Judea and Samaria. The strategy outlined by Jesus of the Apostles being witnesses in Jerusalem first, and then in Judea and Samaria, was being fulfilled not only through the power of the Spirit in the community of the church but also through the reality of persecution. It could be truthfully said that the Apostles stayed in Jerusalem and only made forays initially into the hinterland of Judea and Jerusalem (see Acts 8:1), leaving other members of the church moved by the Spirit to do so. A further irony is added by the fact that the final stage of the mission indicated by Jesus—i.e. going to the ends of the earth (see Acts 1:8)—was accomplished by the very man (Saul/Paul) at whose feet clothes were laid during the physical exertion of stoning Stephen (Acts 7:58). Persecution was very much at the heart of the spread of the Gospel. As the Book of Revelation would make clear, the blood of the martyrs was and is the seed of the church.

## The Samaritans Embraced (Acts 8: 1b-25)

There is little doubt that the Samaritans, even to Jewish Christians, were outsiders. As John tells his readers in explaining the conversation between Jesus and the Woman at the Well, Jews have no dealings with Samaritans (John 4:9b). Samaritans were to the Jews a hybrid race, ethnically mixed (see 2 Kings 17:24ff), spiritually corrupt and fatally compromised, and worse than Gentiles. They were not welcome to Jerusalem or to worship at the Temple, which once they had desecrated. If Greek and Hebrew Jews found it hard enough to get along in caring for their respective widows (Acts 6:1), how much more difficult would Jewish and Samaritan Christians find it to get along. The very early church found it hard to appreciate that all divisions, ethnically and socially, collapsed in Jesus Christ; as Paul wrote, "There is neither Jew nor Greek, slave or Free, male nor female, for you are all one in Christ Jesus" (Galatians 3:28). But God sovereignly overcame all division between Jew and Samaritan, fulfilling Jesus' own prediction to the Woman as the Well that, "You Samaritans worship what you do not know; we worship what we do know, for salvation is from the Jews. Yet a time is coming and has now come when the true worshippers will worship he Father in spirit and truth, for they are the kind of worshippers the Father seeks. God is Spirit, and his worshippers must worship in spirit and truth" (John 4:22–24). That moment was about to arrive not through the Apostles, although Peter and John were sent to Samaria by the Apostles to confirm the inclusion of the Samaritans into the church and to fill them with the Spirit. Rather, it arrived through the ministry of Philip.

Samaritans in Luke's Gospel have a more significant place than in any other Gospel. Mark gives no reference to Samaritans, Matthew tells us only of the prohibition to go a Samaritan town or the Gentiles in his sending out of the Twelve (10:5), and John gives is the account of the telling conversation between Jesus and the Samaritan woman. But Luke tells of Samaritan opposition to Jesus and the disciples because they were passing through Samaria on their way to Jerusalem without stopping (9:52ff). But despite the reaction of James and John to the opposition of the Samaritans, wanting to call down fire on the unwelcoming Samaritan villages, Jesus was content to make a Samaritan the hero of his parable of the same name (the Good Samaritan). It was the Samaritan who was neighbour to the one who fell among thieves, shaming the Priest and the Levite, and the reaction to the parable must have been one of shock and revulsion even amongst Jesus' closest supporters, such was the loathing and contempt amongst Jews for the Samaritans. But even if the mission to the Samaritans in Jesus' own lifetime was curtailed "to the lost sheep of the house of Israel" (Matthew 10:6), Jesus did not restrict his own ministry to the Israelites alone as we have seen. John tells us that Jesus conducted a mini-mission to the residents of Sychar (John 4:39ff) following his conversation with the Woman at the Well. Finally, Luke tells us that Jesus healed ten lepers (17:11ff) on his way to Jerusalem along the border of Samaria and Galilee, one of them was a Samaritan and he only came back to thank Jesus profusely for his healing. Jesus responded by saying, "Were not all ten cleansed? Where are the other nine? Was no-one found to return except this foreigner?". These straws in the wind were indicative of a greater mission to the Samaritans to follow; what Jesus had begun Philip was to complete.

When it comes to the evangelisation of the Samaritans in Acts, it is in some ways strange that it took so long. The day of Pentecost had equipped the church. There were a large number of Christian men and women to draw on to begin the next stage of mission, but the church seemed strangely confined to Jerusalem. Judea was Jerusalem's hinterland, and Samaria was only 40 miles north of Jerusalem, a two days journey by foot. It lay across the main road north from Jerusalem to Galilee and yet it was not until persecution had broken out in Jerusalem that the good news of the Kingdom (Acts 8:12) was first preached in Samaria. It took this persecution to disperse Philip to Samaria, together with other believers, and there he led a dynamic campaign of evangelisation with powerful miracles (8:6–8). As a result of his mission there "was great joy in the city" (8:8). Despite the blemish of Simon Magus who later sought to buy the power of the Spirit, the mission was a great success. But it lacked one essential thing: Philip was only able to baptise the converts in the name of Jesus but without the Apostles' presence, the Samaritan converts could not receive the Holy Spirit and so be fully included in the fellowship of the Church. Clearly the inclusion of the Samaritans on the same terms as the Jews into the united fellowship of the church was an enormous event. Years of enmity and prejudice between Jew and Samaritan were not easily swept aside, it required both an authoritative action by the Apostles but also a sovereign and unmistakeable action of inclusion by God himself, overruling all that had gone before. This is what happened. The Apostles Peter and John, seemingly the leading Apostles of the early Jerusalem church (see also Acts 3:1), were sent down to Samaria, where, upon meeting the new converts, they prayed for them and for the first time they received the Spirit. Their obvious receipt of the Spirit marked their inclusion by God into the church: Jew and Samaritan were now united in their one baptism, one faith, and the one gift of the Spirit. Jerusalem, Judea, and now the Samaritans had been included, it was now time for the rest of the world, the Gentiles.

## The Gentiles Included (Acts 10)

The choreography of the Holy Spirit in enabling the entry of the Gentiles into the Kingdom of God to become joint heirs, with the Jews, of salvation and eternal life was intricate. The intricacy is well shown by Luke in the narrative of Acts where the first Gentiles, the Centurion Cornelius and his household and friends, were included in the church. Once again— despite Jesus' command that after receiving the Spirit the Apostles were to be witnesses in Jerusalem, Judea, Samaria, and the ends of the earth (Acts 1:8)—the Apostles had got little further than Jerusalem, with just occasional forays into Judea and Samaria! It was the Holy Spirit who now sovereignly orchestrated the inclusion of the Gentiles. He had a busy time preparing, convincing, and filling the main actors in the story. It was to be a momentous moment for the world, and it seemed as though all the resources of God in communication were used in overcoming the inertia of human or religious prejudice and of changing the mind-set of Peter.

In the first instance, much of the activity of God centred on Peter and Cornelius and getting them to meet. The inclusion of the Gentiles required: a visit of an Angel to Cornelius to get him to invite Peter; a vision, in preparation for the inclusion of the Gentiles, being given to Peter showing that all foods were clean; the carefully timed arrival of messengers from Cornelius inviting Peter to his house; the direction by the Spirit of Peter to go with them; and the falling of the Spirit on the assembled company in Cornelius house as Peter spoke (see Acts 10). A failure in any of these links in the chain would have resulted, temporarily, in the Gentiles not being included. Once again, the intermingling of the divine with the human makes for almost comic moments. Cornelius, who is another God-fearing Centurion (of which there are a few in the New Testament (see Luke 7:1–10, Mark 15:39, Acts 22:26), is addressed as a God-fearing, prayerful alms-giving man by an angel and literally given his marching orders of sending men to fetch Peter from the home of Simon the Tanner in Joppa. Meanwhile as the messengers approach, Peter falls into a hunger-induced trance in which he sees all kind of food, much of it not kosher, which he is told to eat, despite his protestations of not eating anything "impure" (Acts 10:14)! After this has happened three times, there is knock on the door by three men (10:7–8) and they invite Peter to Cornelius' home. On arrival, Peter was ecstatically received (10:25–26) by Cornelius and Peter politely asked why he had been invited (10:29)! The enthusiasm of Cornelius then drew out of Peter an address in which he showed that "the penny had dropped" and that God does not show favouritism or discrimination but "accepts men from every nation who fear him and does what is right" (10:35). During the course of Peter's address, the Spirit fell on the assembled company. They found themselves filled with Spirit, praising God in their own and other tongues. Peter realised that those whom God had included by the giving them the Spirit should not be refused Baptism, for as he said in his report to the Apostles in Jerusalem about this unplanned (by the Apostles) event: "If God gave them the same gift as he gave us, who believed in the Lord Jesus Christ, who was I to think that I could oppose God" (11:17). God had done through the Spirit what the Apostles had not done because of their innate suspicion: he had included the Gentiles. The Gospel had truly gone to the outsiders.

But what Peter reluctantly had begun, another come-lately Apostle would take on completely. His commission was clear. As God said to Ananias, "This man is my chosen instrument to carry my name before the Gentiles and their Kings and before the people of Israel. I will show him how much he must suffer for my name" (9:15–16). Paul would take on what Peter had begun. His would be the mission to the Gentiles, and Luke would observe how, through Paul's ministry, the Gentiles of the Roman Empire and beyond would be included in the church. For Paul this was the mystery of the Gospel (Ephesians 3:6), how the dividing wall of hostility between Jew and Gentile was abolished (Ephesians 2:14ff). It would engage Paul in extraordinary ministry in the pagan world starting from Antioch and spreading to five other great cities of the Roman world.

The early chapters of Acts shows us a vital, exemplary church in Jerusalem (see especially Acts 2:42–47 and 4:32–37), but one which is still strangely reticent at going outside the city, whether to Samaria or to the Gentiles. It required both the onset of persecution and the conversion of Saul to take the gospel truly to the Gentiles and to the regional centres of power in the Roman Empire.

# CHAPTER 10

# The Tale of Six Cities

Paul was truly the Apostle of the outsider; in his case they could be defined as the Gentiles. After being converted on the road to Damascus, where he was going to arrest the followers of Christ, Paul then spent three years in the desert (Galatians 1:17) before going up to Jerusalem with Barnabas, to meet Peter and James (Galatians 1:18). For the next fourteen years Paul would minister in Syria, his home province of Cilicia, and in Tarsus, his hometown, before being brought by Barnabas to Antioch to instruct the large church there (Galatians 2:1; Acts 11:25–26), which henceforward would become the headquarters for his missionary journeys. If Jerusalem was the centre of the Jewish church, Antioch was the centre of the Gentile Church. Safely settled and supported in this large, mostly Gentile, town, Paul embarked on his missionary journeys. Having pushed into the hinterland north of Antioch, into Galatia and Cappadocia, he was guided by the Spirit to go West and then to the southern Aegean. In a strategic missionary movement he went to all the great centres of population in the Roman Empire except Alexandria. His was a regional strategy in which he planted churches in the great regional cities of the Empire, or strengthened those already planted, such as in Rome. From these regional centres from which government, trade, culture, and commerce spread, the newly founded churches would have ample scope for evangelism from a strong base. Amongst others, his journeys took him to these great regional cities.

# Antioch

Antioch was founded by the successors of Alexander the Great and became a principal city in the region ruled by the Seleucids, founded by Seleucus I Nicator *c.*323 BC. Built at the foot of Mount Silpius, it overlooked the navigable river of the Orontes that flows down through Syria. The city boasted a fine seaport called Seleuchia Pieria, which quickly gave the city great trading possibilities. The city grew rapidly, and by the time of Jesus was one of the three great cities of the Roman Empire, the other two being Rome and Alexandria. Important pagan antiquities bordered or embellished the city: the renowned groves of Daphne, a sanctuary dedicated to Apollo and a fine *agora* (or market place). Its population was nearly half a million; its culture was diverse, cosmopolitan, and rich. Unlike Jerusalem, which was almost monolithically Jewish—boasting the great institution of the Temple—here was a Gentile city of openness and diversity. It was here that the early church especially flourished. What is certain is that the intellectual and spiritual atmosphere of the two cities could not have been more different. Jerusalem hosted the mother church, but Antioch the missionary one.

The founding of the church of Antioch occurred through the dispersion of Christians through persecution (Acts 11:19). It was Christians from Cyprus and Cyrene (Libya), scattered by persecution from Jerusalem, that preached the gospel to the mostly Gentile population of Antioch. We are told that "the lord's hand was with them", for a great number of people believed (11:21). It was a church to rival the size of Jerusalem where three thousand believed in a single day. It was to become the most significant church in the Empire after Rome as one of the five Patriarchates of the early church; it remained very influential until the seventh century when a combination of the Arab invasion and earthquakes diminished its significance as a Christian centre.

In the days of the Apostle Paul, diversity and enthusiasm were evident in its leadership. In the leadership team of the church there were people from Africa (Libya again) and maybe further inland, including a courtier called Manaen who had been brought up with Herod the Tetrarch, the slayer of John the Baptist. It was while they were praying and fasting that the Lord said, "Set apart for me Barnabas and Saul for the work to which I have called them" (13:2), and their missionary work began. The first missionary journey took Paul west to the island of Cyprus, to Salamis and Paphos where the Roman Governor was converted. Paul and his companions then returned to the mainland, to the smaller towns of Galatia, Psidia, and Cappadocia, a region bordering in Paul's home region of Cilicia (see Acts 13 and 14). Paul's second journey began by revisiting the churches founded in the first, but when Paul sought to go further north to Bithynia, bordering the Black Sea, his plans were somehow resisted (16:7–9). The Spirit had other ideas, and while they waited in Troas (not far from the ancient site of Troy or the killing fields of Gallipoli in the First World War) Paul had a vision of a Macedonian man who said, "Come over and help us". From such a simple invitation given in a vision, a mission began which would truly change the face of the world. Paul could not have known where the journey would eventually take him; it was this journey, more than any other, which determined the course of Paul's evangelism for the remainder of his life and the direction of Christian mission towards the very heart of a hostile empire. Paul sailed from Troas, passed the island of Samothrace, to Neapolis, the port of Philippi itself: "from there we travelled to Philippi, a Roman colony and the leading city of that region of Macedonia. And we (notice Luke was with them now) stayed there several days" (16:12). It was not uneventful!

## Philippi

Philippi lies a little inland from the sea and the port of Neaoplis (the present picturesque Greek town of Kavala in Thrace). From here Paul went directly to Philippi, just a few miles inland. Philippi was founded by Philip II of Macedon, the father of Alexander the Great, in 356 BC, hence the city's name. It guarded the route between Amphipolis and Neapolis, and flourished commercially due to nearby gold mines. Later in Roman times it lay on the important road, the *Via Egnatia,* which linked the Adriatic (and hence just a short sea link to Italy) with Byzantium. It was the site of an important battle in the Roman civil war after the assassination of

Julius Caesar. Here Octavian (later Caesar Augustus; see Luke 1:2) and Mark Anthony defeated Brutus and Cassius, the conspirators, at the battle of Philippi in 42 BC. Rich with history, a chief city in Macedonia, rivalled only by Thessalonica, truly Greco-Roman with a strong pagan cultural life, it was to be the home of one of the most lively, good-hearted, and generous churches in the New Testament era. Paul calls them "true partners" in the Gospel (Philippians 1:5ff). He held them in deep affection (1:7–8), remembered how they came to his aid (Philippians 4:15), supporting him from earliest days. They continued their generosity when Paul was as prisoner in Rome (4:18) through Epaphroditus, and they shamed the well intentioned but procrastinating Corinthians into giving (2 Corinthians 8:1ff). They were as near as we can get in the New Testament to a model church. Their beginnings could not have been more extraordinary.

The story is told in Acts 16:11–40. The founding of the church there took Paul and Luke on a visit to a traditional place of prayer (16:13) by the river, where Lydia was found seeking God. God opened her heart to the message of Paul and she believed (16:14b). But as a result of a confrontation with a fortune-teller and the exorcising of her spirit of divination with consequent loss of earning to her owner, a hasty case was brought against Paul and Silas in the context of public unrest and anger at the loss of income to this slave-girl's owner. The magistrates had Paul and Silas flogged and beaten (16:22) and thrown into gaol. An earthquake occurred that night, but Paul and Silas' faith and their concern for the gaoler (16:27, 28) despite their sufferings so impressed him that he and his family believed and were baptised (16:33–34). What an unusual church it must have been: the sophisticated businesswoman Lydia, the gaoler and his family, possibly the slave girl freed from exploitation, and a number of other townsfolk and friends. Only a few days after their arrival, they left with a church formed with minimal follow-up (16:40) but which, under the guidance of the Spirit, became one of the best churches in the New Testament. The Spirit had initiated so much: the call of Paul to Macedonia, the seeking of Lydia at the place of prayer, the confrontation with the fortune-telling slave girl, and the earthquake and the gaoler ready to believe, he presumably could now undertake the maturing of the church after so short a time with Paul.

From Philippi Paul went to Thessalonica, the other principal city of Macedonia also founded by Philip of Macedon and on the *Via Egnatia*. For Paul it was an equally demanding mission. He stayed there for only three weeks, preaching in the synagogues in the face of great opposition from the Jews. It was their fierce opposition to Paul and his preaching which drove him from the town but not before the founding of a church with "some Jews" and "a large number of God-fearing Greeks and not a few prominent women" (17:4). It was also in Thessalonica that the charge was brought by the incensed mob against Jason and other "brothers" that they were defying Caesar's decrees, "saying that there is another King called Jesus" (17:7b): a charge which was to form the kernel of the conflict between the church and the Imperial state of Rome in the centuries to come. However, a church had been founded for which Paul had a special affection; writing of them later he said:

> When we were torn away from you for a short time (in person, not in thought), out of our intense longing we made every effort to see you—certainly I Paul did again and again—but Satan stopped us. For what is our hope, our joy, or crown in which we will glory in the presence of our Lord Jesus Christ when he comes? Is it not you? Indeed, you are our glory and our joy."
>
> *1 Thessalonians 2:18–19*

As he said earlier in the same letter:

> We loved you so much that we were delighted to share not only the Gospel of God but our own lives as well, because you had become so dear to us.
>
> *1 Thessalonians 1:8*

From Thessalonica, Paul went inland into the hills west of the city and came to Berea where the people were "of more noble character" and where Paul's message was received with great eagerness and where they studied the scriptures to see whether what he said was true (Acts 17:11). More Jews believed, as did many Greek men, and once again not a few "prominent women". The future of the church in the Roman Empire often turned on the influence of such women with the authorities. But the mob from Thessalonica turned up at Berea to stir up the people against Paul. Leaving behind Timothy and Silas to encourage the church, Paul and his escort left for the coast and most probably went by ship to Athens.

## Athens

Whether Paul planned on going to Athens originally or whether his arrival there was due the circumstances of his missionary journey so far, we cannot be sure. Luke writes it as though Paul was merely there to wait for Timothy and Silas (17:16). But a visit to the intellectual capital of the ancient world, the centre of Greek culture, which was still at the root of Roman civilisation, would not pass uneventfully in Paul's journey. Rome was *the* Imperial city, the centre of the empire's political and imperial power, but Athens was its intellectual root. What say Oxford and Cambridge are to London in England, Athens was to Rome. It was an outpost of the Empire, but its mother in terms of thought. It was deeply pagan to Paul's Jewish and now Christian monotheistic convictions. It was the home of some of the great philosophies which dominated Greek thought. Its rhetoric and politics formed an intellectual basis for Rome and later the whole of Western culture. Paul's stay at Athens was not therefore just a re-fuelling point in his missionary journey, which would eventually lead to Rome, but made for a profound dialogue and debate between the thought at the root of Greek culture and the essence of the Christian message. Nor was Paul's stay in Athens simply a clash between Jewish or Christian monotheism and plural Greek paganism, it was also a master class in apologetics—how to perceive where your audience is as well as to demonstrate the emptiness of their position and the universal truth of the gospel of Jesus Christ. It is brimful with lessons for the church today.

Firstly, the sheer number of pagan deities found in Athens, seemingly covering every aspect of life, provoked Paul. In fact these shrines and idols greatly distressed him (literally gave him a paroxysm). He was jealous for the honour and name of God. Paul was no stranger to pagan worship. He would have seen temples in Tarsus and Antioch, and in the Roman colonies that he had already visited in Salamis, Paphos, and Galatia. But in Athens it was the sheer number of deities, around every corner, which must have distressed his spirit. Knowing the unity of the godhead, the power and divinity of Father, Son, and Spirit and their transcendence over all creation, this profusion of images, which had no real spiritual power other than the negative one of deception, was extremely provoking to Paul. The result was that he dialogued with the Jews and God-fearing Greeks in the synagogue and with the philosophers and thinkers in the market place (17:17).

Two particular schools of philosophy were well represented in Athens: the Stoics and the Epicureans. Between them they represent two different understandings of life and two approaches to living. The Epicureans or "philosophers of the garden", founded by Epicurus who died in 270 BC, considered the gods to be so remote as to have no influence over human affairs. The world and its existence was due to chance, and there would be no survival of death, and no judgement. So human beings should pursue pleasure, enjoy life to the full, follow sensual pleasure to their hearts' content and be detached from fear, pain, and passion. The Stoics followed quite different ideas. They were not philosophers of the garden but of the porch, the *stoa*, which was the entrance to the *agora* where they taught. They were founded by Zeno who died in 265 BC. He acknowledged the supreme god in a pantheistic type of way, confusing him with the "world soul":

> The world was determined by fate, and human beings must pursue their duty, resigning themselves to live in harmony with nature and reason, however painful his might be, and develop their own self-sufficiency. To oversimplify it; it was characteristic of Epicureans to emphasise chance, escape and the enjoyment of pleasure, and for the Stoics to emphasize fatalism, submission, and the endurance of pain.[82]

These two philosophies are still influential today. Paul was able to argue with them, understanding their philosophies, publicly disputing and dialoguing with them, indeed presenting to them something they had never heard—"the good news of Jesus and the resurrection" (17:18b).

Because of this, Paul was summoned to present his ideas to the Areopagus: a kind of intellectual council that sat in Athens. Having been provoked, having publicly engaged with the Jews, God-fearers, and philosophers, Paul now proclaimed a message to them the like of which they had never heard before; but "since all Athenians and the foreigners who lived there spent their time doing nothing but talking about and listening to the latest ideas" (17:21) Paul was welcome to speak.

Paul's method of preaching was exemplary for any preaching to those outside the Christian faith. He started where they were. He had walked around the town and seen one altar "to the unknown God" (17:23). He told them of this incident, and then said "what you worship as something unknown, I am going to proclaim to you" (17:23). In other words, he began to answer a question that the Athenians themselves had raised. For effective communication with the not-yet Christian world, communicators must start with the questions that their culture has raised. In speaking recently to a whole school event with about a thousand pupils, staff, and parents present, it was only when I used some lyrics about freedom from a well-known folk group who had played recently at the English music festival at Glastonbury that the audience really began to listen. We must be aware of what are the questions that present British culture is asking, and how we might answer them. Having identified this opening to make known the reality of a God whom they do not yet know, Paul then began to proclaim to them who he is.

The message, which Paul proclaimed to these would-be philosophers of the Areopagus, was that their gods were far too small, and indeed were no gods at all. The unknown God whom the Athenians name-checked at a temple as being "the unknown god", Paul now declared to them. He was the creator: he is "the God who made the world and everything in it" and is "the Lord of heaven and earth", and consequently cannot be housed in a little temple in Athens (17:24), nor is he "served by human hands as he himself sustains everything". He was also the creator of human life, creating life and breath and the human family with its own territory. Although God cannot be blamed for national arrogance or aggression, he is nonetheless in control of all nations and their future, and, as the writer of Ecclesiastes says, has put eternity in the heart of man with the consequent desire of people seeking after God to find him (see Ecclesiastes 3:11). Quoting again from Epimenides, a sixth-century pagan poet from Crete, he said "in him we live and move and have our being";[83] so God is not only transcendent but immanent—above us and around us. Furthermore, as a third-century Stoic poet said from Paul's home province of Cilicia, "we are his offspring"[84] (17:28): that is we are made in his image with the result that, as Augustine later said, "our hearts are restless till they find their rest in thee."[85] So Paul uses two pagan poets to further his message God's greatness and proximity.

But then the surprise came. Since we are his offspring, God cannot be a lump of stone or precious metal or intricately worked object without life or power. After all he has created us, giving us life and breath and therefore he must be greater than us, and anything we could make. And if he is unlike all these images set up to represent him in Athens or anywhere else, then people must change their minds and hearts especially since this great Creator will come to be our Judge. But the proof of this judgement to come, and here is the surprise, is that he has sent a *man* who has not only returned from death to life but is the one who will be the judge of all human offspring. In Athens it was the resurrection that Paul especially seemed to preach (17:18b) to demonstrate the creative sovereignty of God and his supremacy over all things, and, no doubt, to make his hearers ask who was this one who conquered death and who would judge the world. No wonder some said "we want to hear you again on this" and several believed (17:32). If the preaching of Creation and the Resurrection was centre stage in Athens, when he came to Corinth it was the preaching of the Cross.

## Corinth

Paul's next recorded stopping place on this missionary journey was Corinth: a short journey, probably by sea, from Athens. He was to stay there at least 18 months. On arrival he met a Christian couple, Aquila and Priscilla, recently come from Rome from where they and other Christians had been expelled by an edict of the Emperor Claudius due to religious disturbances between Jews and Christians. They were tentmakers and as Paul himself was a tentmaker, which had been his family business, he worked with them to make a living whilst teaching in the synagogue. But soon an abusive reaction to his proclamation of Jesus being the Messiah set in so that he shook out his clothes at them, a sign of formal judgement on their refusal to accept his message, and he left the synagogue for the Gentiles (18:67b). As usual, he began by preaching to the Jews in the Synagogue until there was violent reaction. Paul then solemnly left the synagogue and went to the Gentiles. But his preaching had not been fruitless: Crispus, one of the synagogue rulers, believed, and, together with his entire household, was baptised. And many other Corinthians also believed. It was at this point that the Lord appeared to him in a dream encouraging him to stay, "For I have many people in this city" (18:10). Paul stayed a further 18 months "teaching them the word of God" (18:11).

During the visit to Athens, Paul concentrated on preaching God as Creator and Judge, and the Resurrection of Jesus was used to confirm this teaching (17:18b, 17:31), while in Corinth, especially at the outset, he concentrated his teaching on the Cross. So in his first Epistle to the Corinthians Paul recalls that when he first came to the city: "He resolved to know nothing while I was with you except Jesus Christ and him crucified" (1 Corinthians 2:2), and he recalled that he arrived "in weakness and fear and trembling" (1 Corinthians 2:3). So why did he seemingly focus on Creation and the new Creation, as borne witness to by the Resurrection, in Athens, whereas in Corinth he seemed more concentrated on preaching the death of Jesus on the cross? Could there be any explanation in the culture of the respective cities that drew the particular teaching from Paul? In Athens they had no idea of the universal authority of God in creation and judgement which in turn was demonstrated by the resurrection of Jesus from the dead. In Corinth, on the other hand, it seems that they had no idea that God revealed his wisdom and salvation in weakness and suffering. The culture in one city drew out one set teachings from the gospel while the culture in another city, not far distant but with a distinctly different past and culture, drew out a very different emphases from the same gospel. Athens was very much the University City, remaining so until the fifth century, while Corinth was a commercial centre for the successful businessman who had money to spend and pleasure to seek.

It is case of allowing the culture of a city to determine the teaching or preaching that is given.

As in Philippi, Paul did not escape without one court appearance. But here the outcome was different. The proconsul to whose court he was hauled was Gallio, the proconsul of Achaia (18:12ff), but since Gallio saw this complaint as a purely religious dispute about Jewish words, doctrines, and names, he threw out the case telling them to settle it themselves. In the future, Roman courts would be less dismissive of Christian matters as they came to see the preaching of Christ as Lord as a threat to the hegemony of the Empire and the divine authority of the Emperor. Not revering the Emperor as divine and not taking an oath to him would become a treasonable offence, and Christians would pay for such treason with their lives. The courtroom appearances or interaction with the authorities of Paul in Philippi, Corinth, Ephesus, Caesarea, and Rome make an interesting study, but what we see in general terms is that after their initial duty of keeping the peace between Jew and Christian, or pagan practice and Christian monotheism, the courts come to enforce the claim of the Emperor to be divine over against this new Jewish sect which would only agree to Jesus being the Lord. No conversation was probably possible between the proconsul in Achaia and the City Clerk who dispersed the crowd in Ephesus (19:35), but, had there been, one wonders what might have been its content. After returning fleetingly via Ephesus to Antioch, Paul, as he had promised, returned to Ephesus on his third journey and once again found a city with another powerful pagan culture in opposition to the gospel.

# Ephesus

Ephesus was a great regional city in the Eastern Mediterranean with a population in the first century AD of around 200,000. Paul visited it on his way back to Antioch at the end of his second missionary journey. He went there with Priscilla and Aquila, with whom he had worked in Corinth. Paul then left them there, promising to return (18:26), while he went to report how he had got on to the church in Antioch; but he soon returned near the beginning of his third missionary journey having visited Galatia. (18:20 and 19:1). The culture in Ephesus was dominated by the cult of Diana or Artemis, whose temple on the perimeter of the city was one of the great wonders of the world; only a single pillar of it still remains. But the city was full of temples and elegant houses and shopping arcades. The great Amphitheatre dominated Harbour St, which ran from the sea into the city. It gave an impressive approach to the city which Paul, like all travellers arriving by sea, would have experienced.

But the religious life of the city was dominated by the worship of Artemis and further influenced by occult practice and Jewish exorcists who in one case failed to exorcise a man who beat them up instead (19:16)! Alongside the many miracles, power encounters between light and darkness, and demonstrations of the authority of Jesus (19:11–12), Paul proclaimed the message firstly in the synagogue and then in the lecture hall of Tyrannus where he argued every day for the Kingdom. So effective was the ministry and so many turned both from occult practises and the worship of Artemis that it challenged the trade of the silversmiths and other craftsmen in the making of silver replica shrines for pilgrims. A silversmith called Demetrius addressed the tradesmen in the Amphitheatre, a riot ensued, Paul's companions Gaius and Aristarchus were seized, and Paul himself was warned off from going into the theatre for fear of his life, and only the emollient words of the city clerk restrained their fury and dispersed the crowd. Paul had stirred a spiritual hornets' nest, but a church of some size had been founded which would soon welcome the Apostle John as its leader (c.AD 65), who would remain amongst them until his death after exile in Patmos.[86]

The ministry in Ephesus was not dissimilar in length from that in Corinth but it had a distinctive nature of its own given the culture and the spirituality of the city. But by now common features were emerging in Paul's ministry in all these regional centres: firstly, engagement with the Jews and God-fearers in the synagogues until, almost without exception, Paul was thrown out having made a few converts; engagement in Athens, Corinth, and Ephesus with pagan philosophical opinions; encounters with occult practises, whether in Philippi (the fortune telling slave girl) or Ephesus (a trade in occult publications and the Jewish exorcists); and finally conflict with the authorities in Philippi, Thessalonica, Corinth, and Ephesus. These were the ingredients of Paul's missions along with miraculous healing (see Acts 19:11–12 and Romans 15:18–19) and powerful proclamation of the gospel with an emphasis on those parts of the gospel which were especially pertinent to the spiritual, moral, and social outlook of the community in which he was speaking. In these ways he ministered to the outsider, to the Gentile, to the Jew who would listen, and to those enmeshed in pagan philosophy and religion.

## Rome

Finally, Paul arrived in Rome after his long and eventful sea voyage from Caesarea in Palestine (Acts 27:2), via Crete, shipwreck at Malta, Sicily, and the toe of Italy. Paul had already written his most lengthy letter to the church in Rome probably towards the end of his third missionary journey when in Greece (see Acts 20:3). The church in Rome had probably come into existence during the reign Emperor Claudius (AD 41–54), the successor of Caligula who had been assassinated and who was the predecessor to Nero. The church was established in Rome by the movement of Christians to the capital of the Empire as a result of trade or family ties.

The frequency of travel in the Empire is made clear in the narrative of Priscilla and Aquila's lives. As Jewish Christians they were expelled from Rome on the orders of Claudius in AD 49 (as recorded by his secretary Suetonius in his *Claudius 25*, where Jews were blamed for causing religious riots in Rome, "on account of one Chrestus", almost certainly Christ). They were first met by Paul in Corinth after their expulsion (Acts 18:2). They then moved to Ephesus to help Paul, and remained there when he returned to Antioch at the end of the second Missionary journey (Acts 18:19, 26). But they are also mentioned in the long list of people greeted by Paul at the end of his epistle to the Romans (see Romans 16:3ff) only a little time later. In a few years they had moved from Rome to Corinth, to Ephesus and then back to Rome.

When Paul arrived in Rome at the end of his eventful voyage accompanied by Luke (Acts 27:1ff), he was received by an already well established church in about AD 61. The Emperor was now Nero. Paul was initially placed under arrest and free to receive guests (Acts 28:30–31). He remained in detention for two years, may then have been released during which time he may have visited the Aegean and Spain. He was then probably re-arrested by Nero when the persecution of Christians intensified after the great fire of Rome in AD 64, when the Christians were made scapegoats for this disaster. It was during this period that Paul wrote his prison letters to the Philippians (Philippians 1:12–14), the Ephesians (Ephesians 3:1), the Colossians (Colossians 4:18), and Timothy (2 Timothy 4:6ff). His influence was as great in this moving prison correspondence penned from Rome as his ministry to the church in Rome, a church already well formed and mature. His ministry was as much to the church at large as to the church in Rome itself, although his presence there could not have been anything other than inspiring to the Roman Christians.

But Acts closes with the great Apostle to the Gentiles at the heart of the Gentile world, in the capital of the Empire. As in the gospel Jesus moved from his birthplace, Bethlehem to Galilee and then inevitably to Jerusalem, so Paul moved from Tarsus to Jerusalem and Antioch, and inevitably eventually to Rome. Just as a prophet could not perish away from Jerusalem, so the Apostle to the Gentiles world could not but end his earthly days in Rome. It was a natural culmination of Paul's ministry to the Gentile, to the outsider; his life was truly sacrificed for them.

CHAPTER 11

# The Gospel for the Outsider

A few years ago we had an important decision to take about the shape of our future ministry as a church: in short, it was whether to start a new venture in reaching out to a group of youngsters, some of whom were on the very edge of school, society, and crime, or whether to keep to the safe confines of our existing ministry. We had been studying St Luke's Gospel for some time and had been considering some of the themes we have looked at in this book; but it was not an easy decision. It would need new funding, a dedicated community youth worker, and a team of volunteers, a long commitment in the same direction as Eugene Peterson puts it when describing discipleship and no doubt many ups and downs for the team along the way.[87] I am glad to say the Church Council decided, after some necessary heart-searching, to go ahead, and the last three years since that decision have been exciting, demanding, and at times exhausting ones for those on the front line. It began with two of the leaders simply sitting on a bench outside the local chippy and engaging young people in conversations before providing different kinds of meetings for them to come to: one called the *Den* with activities, another called *check it out* to engage with spiritual questions they might have, another teaching life skills from photography to cooking. A group of them went to Malawi for an intensive two weeks of interaction with a rural development programme called Eagles, with a street kids charity, with a lively African church, and with some remarkable field workers in these charities. Few of the group had been outside of the UK before, let alone to Africa! It was a life-changing experience. One of them has since become an intern in this work called the *Enrich Youth Project*, and a few others spent a week at Soul

Survivor. They would not necessarily say they are all the way there with the Christian faith yet; but the journey continues. The aim of the project is "to love young people towards wellbeing and the understanding of God's goodness". It is an on-going attempt to go outside the confines of normal church; to take the church into the community not the community into the church. As such it is like many, many projects around the country which seek through venturesome love to go outside the church. Firstly, who are the outsiders?

## Outsiders Today

There are many different ways and levels of answering this question. In one sense, Christians are the outsiders, exiles and strangers in the world (see 1 Peter 1:1) : here for a time but with no abiding home, sojourners in the world as the Epistle to Diognetus says: "they [Christians] dwell in their own country but simply as sojourners".[88] In the stories told by Luke in his Gospel, the outsiders were the non-Jew, the sinner, the poor, the diseased, like the leper or the woman with the flow of blood, those in sinful or dubious occupations, like a tax collector or prostitute, sometimes women and certainly pagans and Gentiles. All these were outsiders in Jesus' day.

The outsider today in the UK could be an immigrant, a Muslim, a Jew or a Hindu, a member of a minority or a person ostracised by their peers because of some perceived difference whether sexual, cultural, physical, or mental. It is easy to be thrown by meeting someone very different to yourself and not knowing quite how to respond. I remember sitting in a café in Bristol having a coffee when a man came and sat on the adjoining table whose body and face seemed to be completely covered in tattoos. He sat down next to me and I examined my own reaction. It was a mixture of perplexity and horror: how could anyone do that to themselves, what kind of inner turmoil produced it, how could I engage with him normally (at least in my thoughts) without excluding him. The challenge was to go beyond focussing merely on the tattoos, especially those on his face, and seek the real person within forming a relationship with him. I don't think he was looking to strike up a conversation, but I did wonder how I would approach it: presumably begin with the weather and move on!

I am reminded of the Jewish philosopher Martin Buber whose relational philosophy revolves around an *i:thou* axis rather than *i:it*. He says a choice is always open to us with people: either to enter into a positive relationship with someone who may be similar to or quite unlike yourself; or alternatively withdrawing because of fear (even phobia), intimidation, prejudice, or misunderstanding into an *i:it* relationship in which the person is either made into stereotype or an object (*it*) to be excluded, ignored, or even abused.[89]

It is worth asking yourself *why* we react to people in the way that we do and what are the reasons for doing so. When it is not positive, is our reaction out of concern for our security, or out of resentment or bitterness; for instance, if we know a person and have been hurt by them, or simply feeling awkward and out of our depth, like when meeting a person recently bereaved or who has suffered news of real loss. If these are our reactions then they may prevent us from forming a positive relationship; and if we fail to do that we exclude them. If this ever becomes the case, what are the things which can help us to overcome those attitudes of exclusion, and like Jesus, go out to the outsider?

## Confident of Our Identity

Once our Diocesan Bishop, Peter Price, was asked about what things prevent the church from effectively embarking in mission, or going out to those who as yet are outside God's Kingdom, and bear no allegiance to the King, rather spurning him. He wisely responded that it is when we ourselves know that we are loved and are secure in that knowledge that we can confidently and trustingly join with him in the mission of God (*missio dei*). In other words, we need to be confident and secure in the knowledge of God's love for us.

At the outset of his mission Jesus was baptised and this event is recorded in each of the gospels. Luke tells us, "Jesus was baptised too. And as he was praying, heaven was opened and the Holy Spirit descended on him in bodily form like a dove. And a voice came from heaven: 'you are my Son, whom I love: with you I am well pleased'" (Luke 3:21–22). In fact three actions happened at his baptism. Firstly, Jesus himself identified with the mission of the Father who had sent him into the world (see John 20:21) to declare the Kingdom of God and to die for human sin and rise again. He identified with sinful or broken humankind by being baptised. John's baptism was one of repentance, but Jesus had no sin from which he needed to turn (and because of this John was reluctant to baptise him; see Matthew 3:13), so why was he baptised? He was baptised so as to identify with the humanity he had come to save; it was a baptism which began with water and ended with redemptive suffering (see Mark 10:38)—a baptism of suffering which culminated in being immersed in the "waters" of crucifixion and death. The second aspect of Jesus' baptism was being anointed with the Spirit who came upon him like a dove. He was immeasurably filled with the Spirit. As Gregory of Nyssa wrote: "All that the Father is we see revealed in the Son: all that is the Son's is the Father's also: for the whole Son dwells in the Father and he has the whole Father dwelling in himself".[90] Crafted to defend the divinity of the Son in the face of the Arian controversy in the fourth century, Gregory might well have added, *and it is the Spirit who, as the bond of love between Father and Son, does this*. It is the Spirit who empowered the Son for ministry, and this occurred at his baptism. Thirdly, the Father declared his love for the Son at his baptism: "You are my Son whom I love: with you I am well pleased". Only then did Jesus embark on the mission on which the Father had sent him and for which he had given himself, sure in the knowledge of his Father's love. So this had prepared Jesus for the rigours of his ministry threefold event.

If Jesus was thus equipped for his mission, then similar identification with the task, empowering for the work and reassurance of the Father's pleasure must be ours as well.

## Learning to Listen

If we are to engage with the outsider we must listen in the widest sense of that word; that is, we must hear both what is said and what is left unsaid, as well as what may be discerned by appearance, culture, and body language. Our tendency is to jump too quickly to conclusions or make judgments about a person on the barest of presenting evidence when we do not know what circumstances, trials, or setbacks someone may have faced. Listening and observation are the only means by which we may find out what motivates, controls, or inhibits a person, and only *attentive* listening can reveal what those things might be. Good listening proceeds from trust, when the other person perceives that you are not there to judge them but to hear them out. To do this may require reflective listening, when in short summaries we say what someone has already said and show not only that they have been heard but also that we have registered *accurately* what has been said *and* the emotion with which it has been said (i.e. empathy).

Jesus was a good listener: as a boy he listened carefully in the Temple to the teachers of the Law (Luke 2:46). He listened to the Woman at the Well, to Nicodemus, and to the questions of his own disciples (see Philip in John 14). However, he was far from a passive listener: often his responses were incisive, sharp and challenging as with Nicodemus (see John 3:3), or the rich young ruler (Luke 18:18ff). After all, most of us listen to discover the thoughts and emotions of another that are critical in their thinking, but often Jesus knew without being told. His knowledge was not as dependent as ours is on listening. He listened but often he already knew. He listened but he responded too. He combined wisdom with knowledge: the wisdom to listen but the insight to challenge someone with great clarity. This blend of attentive listening and clear direction is a healing mixture.

Listening is in itself powerful; it enables a release of anxiety and can unlock both hope and possibilities of dealing with the issues facing someone. I think of a Head Teacher of a primary school dealing with some intractable pastoral problems in some of her pupils, whether it is aggressive behaviour, inappropriate language, or unwillingness to co-operate. There may be no short term quick-fix solution, but listening to the issues can help the person responsible to think around the problem, feel supported, and possibly find the energy to continue to face the issues and seek solutions. I think of a retired minister facing the prospect of his wife become deeply affected by Alzheimer's, threatening the quality of their marriage, the hopes for their retirement, and their future social life. Once again, listening and prayer enables hope, lances some of the acute despair, and provides renewed energy to live with alongside a distressing illness.

There is no doubt that Jesus listened but then decisively acted to heal, to restore, and to challenge, but often to listen we must cross the road.

## Crossing the Road

Luke, more than any other Gospel writer, gives us the metaphor of crossing or running down the road to welcome another. I am thinking of his two most famous parables which Jesus told and which only Luke records. Think how impoverished our understanding would be of both the generosity of God and what it means to love our neighbour without the parables of the Prodigal Son and the Good Samaritan. In one, the principal character crosses the road (or at least does not pass by on the other side), and in the other the waiting father runs down road to embrace his returning, penitent, dishevelled son (see Luke 10:34 and 15:20). To the Samaritan, the one who fell among thieves was a complete outsider, but that day this man fell into the orbit of the Samaritan's care—or in Jesus' language, became a neighbour to the Good Samaritan. To the father, his prodigal son was not in a strict sense an outsider but he had become estranged from his father, even lost (see 15:24).

Engaging with outsiders means changing our position. It could be mean abandoning our theological defences. Do not misunderstand me: this does not mean leaving behind God's standards. But it may mean closely identifying and associating with those who are a long way from living close to those standards themselves. After all, the parables of lost and found in Luke 15 were precipitated by Jesus socialising with and welcoming those of dubious morals or those well outside the pale of Jewish orthodoxy (see

15:1–2). To go to outsiders is potentially dangerous, but grace was never safety-first or risk-free, and is always open to misunderstanding and the charge of selling orthodoxy cheap.

## Walking alongside and explaining

Luke is fond of the theme of journey in his writings. He charts the journey of Jesus walking and ministering in Galilee before he resolutely heads south to Jerusalem through the indifference and hostility of Samaria (Luke 9:51). He is the one who gives us the missionary journeys of Paul who takes us from Jerusalem to Rome, from the religious centre of Judaism to the imperial capital of the Western World. But maybe, and most memorably of all, it is Luke who records the journey from Jerusalem to Emmaus where Jesus, unrecognised, joins the two disciples who are mourning the loss of Jesus: "we had hoped that he was the one who was going to redeem Israel" (a play on Zechariah's words "Praise be to the Lord, the God of Israel because he has come and has redeemed his people"; 1:68). The walk continues in delicious irony as Jesus explains the necessity of the Messiah dying and the reader wants to shout out to Cleopas and his friend like a pantomime audience "he is beside you!" But only when their eyes are opened at the breaking of bread did they recognise Jesus and reflected that "were not our hearts burning within us while he talked with us on the road?" (24:32).

So Jesus "walked alongside them" (24:15b), and as he did so he explained from the scriptures (see 24:27). Indeed, explaining the scriptures lies at the heart of Luke's account of Jesus' mission and this is well summarised in the resurrection appearance in the Upper Room (24:33) where we are told "[Jesus] showed them his hands and feet", ate fish and then "opened their minds so that they could understand the scriptures" (24:45). Thereafter Peter explained the scriptures on the day of Pentecost (explaining Joel's prophecy; Acts 2:16ff), Philip explained the scriptures to the Ethiopian eunuch in his chariot (Acts 8:34–35), and Paul repeatedly explained from the scriptures to Jewish audiences that Jesus was the Christ (see Acts 13:16ff).

Walking alongside someone and explaining the scriptures in the context of life is the pattern here, and surely the example that Jesus gives us in the Gospel of how to make known his Kingdom to others: walking with someone and explaining to them *not in a them-and-us kind of way* but as fellow pilgrims seeking the meaning and significance of life is what Jesus himself modelled. Walking and explaining is a good way of collapsing all the barriers between insider and outsider and opening the Kingdom to all.

## Your Kingdom Come

Arguably more powerfully than any other Gospel writer, Luke had the idea of the coming Kingdom uppermost in his narrative and theology. If Matthew showed the coming of the new community of the church heralding the Kingdom of Heaven, Mark showed the authority of Jesus as the new King. If John demonstrated the gift of eternal life as the reward of faith in the divine *logos* come in the flesh, Luke shows us the universal plan of God to bring the message of forgiveness to all people through the work of Jesus and the gift of the Spirit. As his is a two volume work in which the Gospel starts as pinprick in the womb of Mary (1:35) but ends just 40 years later growing in the capital of the Empire where Paul "boldly and without hindrance preached the Kingdom of God and taught about the Lord Jesus Christ" (Acts 28:31), Luke is able to show the march of the Kingdom in his own lifetime from Bethlehem to Rome. Its message is that no one is outside the sweep of this Kingdom's presence. It was announced by Jesus at Nazareth and was experienced by a thief on the cross who said, "Jesus remember me when you come into your kingdom" (23:42). This Kingdom embraced the poor, the leper, the Gentile, the demonised, the untouchable woman, the prostitute, and the rich man. All of these people and many others are found jostling to touch, speak with, and be healed by Jesus. And the parables recorded by Luke, maybe more than any other, depict a merciful, lavishly generous, unstuffy, but

searingly radical Father: the response to whom is best characterised by
the prayer of the Tax Collector in the Temple who said, standing afar off
beating his breast, "God be merciful to me a sinner" (18:13c). He was
the one who went home "justified"; like the prodigal who said he was no
more worthy to be called his father's son; both were swept up in embrace
and exultation of the Father. What better place then for any of us to begin
than with the Jesus Prayer, which surely has the Tax Collector's prayer as
its inspiration: "Jesus Christ, Son of God, have mercy on me a sinner". On
this basis, because of the unspeakable generosity of God, every outsider
is acceptable: that is Luke's gospel for the outsider.

STUDY   1

# Outsiders at the Birth of Christ

## Luke 1:5–80

We will compare the responses of Zechariah and Mary to the news that both would have a child born as a result of God's intervention in their lives. I have characterised Mary as *the outsider*: a young, relatively poor teenage mother suddenly finding herself pregnant outside of marriage. Conversely, I have characterised Zehariah as *the insider*: a member of the priesthood with duties in the Temple, a more mature man who, with Elizabeth, had led a godly life (1:6). Do you think, for the purposes of this study and the thesis of the book, that this is a fair characterisation?

- How would you describe the reactions of Zechariah and Mary to the news that they will have a child (see 1:13–20 and 1:29–38)? Is there any reason as to why they responded differently to the message of Gabriel?
- How does the song of Mary express the theme of Luke's gospel? In what sense is it a charter for the Gospel (see 1:46ff)? Zechariah's song combines praise and prophecy in equal measure; what is striking about this father prophesying at his son's circumcision (the equivalent of baptism in the New Testament)?

## Luke 2:1–52

- In a very real sense Jesus himself became the outsider in Bethlehem: not wanted in the inn, he was wrapped in simple cloths and placed in a manger. What was God's wisdom in this?

- Shepherds and Wise Men were the first to visit Jesus in the stable: why were they chosen to be the first to worship the Christ-child? What message does that convey?
- Two pensioners, Simeon and Anna, first saw the Christ-child in the Temple: why was that? What did they have in common apart from their age?
- What is the overall message for you from the Nativity, as recorded in Luke?

# STUDY 2

# The Manifesto at Nazareth

## Luke 4:14–28

- What was the importance of this occasion?
- Why did Jesus announce his mission and manifesto in his hometown?
- How would you summarise what Jesus had come to do?
- How would you describe the atmosphere in the Synagogue after Jesus sat down (see 4:20–21)? Why did the mood change (contrast 4:22 and 4:28)?
- Why did the congregation get increasingly annoyed and then enraged?
- What tipped them over the age and why (4:28)?
- What caused the resentment in his home congregation?
- Why is a prophet not recognised in his hometown?
- Should we have clear mission statements for our churches today? What kind of things would go into yours if you do not have one? What kind of process should there be to get ownership and agreement?
- What else have you learnt from this passage?

S T U D Y   3

# Encounters with Outsiders

Most of the encounters described in this chapter come from Jesus' Galilean ministry and from two events in the final weeks of Jesus ministry in and around Jericho before he finally comes to Jerusalem. We will look at these encounters in two blocks: the Galilean encounters and the Jericho encounters, encompassing the six meetings with Jesus.

## The Galilean Encounters

There are four in this chapter: with a paralytic (Luke 5:17–26), a centurion (7:1–10), a sinful woman (7:36–50), and the Gerasene demoniac (8:26–39). You may wish to read these accounts again as a group or individually, and, having done so, consider these questions.

- Are there any features in common in these encounters, either in the way Jesus handles them or in the people themselves?
- If you were to draw a chief characteristic in each of these encounters, what would they be?
- What would be the chief testimony of the Paralytic, the Centurion, the sinful woman, and the demoniac, do you think?
- What do these encounters teach us about Jesus?

## The Jericho Encounters

Shortly before his passion and crucifixion, Jesus had two memorable encounters around Jericho with Bartimaeus and Zacchaeus (see 18:35ff and 19:1ff).

- What are the chief contrasts between these stories, and what is so striking about Jesus' conversation with each individual?
- In both cases the crowds did not want Jesus to engage with them; why was that? What is so similar about these stories?
- Summarise what you have learnt from these encounters

S T U D Y   4

# The Parables and Outsiders

We will compare and contrast three of Luke's great parables which contain significant stories about outsiders. They are the parables of the Good Samaritan (Luke 10:25-37), the Prodigal Son (15:11-32), and the Pharisee and Tax Collector (18:9-14). The group might wish to read all three parables together and then answer the following questions.

- Are there any common themes running through these parables? If so, what are they?
- What do the Priest and the Levite, the older brother and the Pharisee have in common?
- What were the shock-factors in each of the parables?
- Why do we find the Prodigal Son more attractive than the older brother?
- What do the Good Samaritan and the Tax Collector have in common?
- What does Jesus want to teach us about the Father, about ourselves, and about our responsibilities in these parables?
- What kind of spirituality is commended by these parables? What values are found in this spirituality: e.g. honesty, realism, humility, compassion?
- Where do we see these values at work in the parables?
- Is there anything else you have seen looking at these parables together?

STUDY   5

# Women as Outsiders

If you have read the chapter in the book, would you go as far as saying that there is a feminine spirituality in St Luke's gospel? You may say, what is a feminine spirituality? My answer would be that it is comprised of characteristics true of women in the Gospel which make their response identifiably different from that of men. In the course of the Gospel I identified five distinguishing features of women's response to either Jesus or the Father.

The five stories taken from the Gospel comprised: Mary (attentive listening; Luke 10:38–42), the widow in the parable of the Unjust Judge (Persistence; 18:1–8), the widow at the Temple treasury (sacrificial giving; 21:1–2), the woman with the jar of perfume in Simon's house (extravagant love; 7:36–50), and the obedient faith of Mary (1:26–38). If there is time, members of the group might read each of these five stories and then discuss their characteristics.

- What does this group of women have in common?
- What can men learn from them?
- Why, in general terms, do the men have a worse press in the Gospel? e.g. dispute amongst the disciples as to which is the greatest (22:24–29), the denial by Peter (22:54–62), and the initial unbelief by Zechariah (1:5–25). Why do men find it so difficult? There are some glorious exceptions, e.g. the Centurion and John the Baptist (see 7:1–10 and 7:18–35).
- Why is it generally true that men like arranging structures, controlling the finances, and speaking from the front, and women caring for the weak, praying for the Kingdom to come, and offering their time, energy, and money in service?
- How do you think Luke regarded women in his Gospel?

# The Gospel and the Poor

If Luke collected a number of stories of Jesus' ministry among women, he no less collected teaching, parables, and stories of meetings with people which revolved around money. More than any other Gospel writer, he highlighted issues of money in discipleship, and did so through a combination of reporting Jesus' teaching on the subject, parables, and encounters with people for whom it was a big issue.

## Teaching

Luke 6:17–26.

- What principles does Jesus establish about wealth? What are its risks, what are its opportunities?

## Parables

Dives and Lazarus (16:19–31); the Rich Fool (12:13–21); the Shrewd Manager (16:1–15); Ten Minas (19:11–27).

If there is time, read around these passages and consider these questions:

- What do they teach about the responsibilities, pitfalls, and opportunities of wealth?

- Why did Jesus commend the shrewd manager? What can we learn from him?
- What should have the Rich Fool and Dives done?
- What does the parable of the Ten Minas teach?

## Encounters around the issue of wealth

The Rich Young Ruler (18:18–30); Zacchaeus (19:1–10).

- Why was one able to give away most his wealth and the other could not? What does that say about the power of wealth and the motives that can release it for others? What perspective does Jesus bring to the money-makers of today's world?
- Summarise what you have learnt from this study

# The Spirit and the Kingdom

Luke has the most developed idea of the Kingdom of God among the
Gospel writers, at the heart of which is, for humanity, salvation through
the forgiveness of sins and a renewed world (see Luke 1:77, 4:43, 5:17b,
9:11b, 23:42–43, 24:47). Both in his parables and actions of healing,
forgiveness, and deliverance, Jesus was making known the Kingdom and
did so through the power of the Spirit.

## The Kingdom

- What do you understand by the Kingdom of God? How is the
  church related to it? In what ways had Jesus come to inaugurate
  the Kingdom of God here on earth?
- How did Jesus show his Kingship? What were the marks of his
  Kingship?
- What role did the disciples have in making known the Kingdom
  (see 9 1–6, 10:1–24)? How can the Kingdom be made known today?

## The Spirit

- Luke also has a deep understanding of the work of the Spirit in
  mission. What is the relationship of the Spirit to Jesus in Luke's
  Gospel, and how did he equip the church for Mission (see Acts
  1:8, 2:1–13)?

- Look at Luke 24:45–53 and Acts 1:4–8: what did these verses mean for the disciples then and what do they indicate to us today? What happens what the Spirit fills the church, what happens he fills an individual? What happened when the Spirit filled Jesus without measure (see Luke 3:22)?
- What do you think is the relationship between the Spirit and the Kingdom?

STUDY 8

# Outsiders at the Passion, Crucifixion and Resurrection

## Luke 22, 23, 24

Read Luke's Passion narrative as a whole, with members of the group reading a paragraph or episode each.

- Who were the outsiders in the story and why?
- Some were attracted to Jesus, others were repelled: why did people in the story react so differently?
- Who comes out of the story well, and who badly, and why?
- What forces were at work in the story and how do they present themselves?
- What are the clues in the passage that tell us how Jesus was thinking?
- In what way does Luke present Jesus as saviour?
- How does Luke present Jesus as the Risen Lord to his readers?
- What is Jesus at pains to explain to his disciples? Why does Jesus put understanding before experience in the Emmaus story and in the Upper Room ?

Re-read the account if there is time with maybe a lighted candle and appropriate music, and listen to the account again. End with prayer.

STUDY 9

# Jerusalem, Judea, Samaria, and the Gentiles

In preparation for this study you might ask the group to read beforehand the first ten chapters of Acts.

As we have seen, the dynamic in the Acts is the continuation of the ministry of Jesus through the church, in the power of the Spirit. So Luke refers Theophilus to what Jesus *began to do* in his own ministry, but now continues to do through the church once the Spirit has been poured out (see Acts 1:1, "what he began to do and teach"). Now the action and teaching of Jesus continues through the Spirit after Pentecost: "when the Spirit comes down the church goes out". The mandate Jesus gave the early church was that "when the Spirit comes upon me you will be my witnesses in Jerusalem and in all Judea and Samaria, and to end of the earth" (1:8).

- How do you understand Pentecost, how does Luke understand it? What difference did and does it make to you?
- What do we mean by a "personal Pentecost"?
- How exciting were the early days of ministry in Jerusalem (see Acts 3–5)? What were the main features of the Apostles' ministry?
- What were the main features of the church's life? Can it or should it be the same today (see 2:42–47, 4:32–37)?
- Do you think the church was bound too much to Jerusalem?
- What precipitated the mission to Samaria (see 8:1–8)?
- Why did Peter need so much convincing to go to the Gentiles and so much "footwork" by the Holy Spirit (see Acts 10)?
- What are our blind-spots in mission in our community? How has the Holy Spirit encouraged you?

STUDY    10

# The Tale of Six Cities

Once again, ask the group to read through Acts 13–19, which covers the six cities (except Rome). As they do, ask them to bear in mind the different settings for the preaching of the Gospel in each city.

- In what ways was the preaching of the Gospel different in each of these cities? In what ways was it the same? What made the preaching different in these cities? e.g. compare Philippi with Ephesus, and Athens and Corinth.
- What were the principal themes of Paul's preaching in Athens and why was that?
- How did they differ to his preaching in Corinth (see 1 Corinthians 2:1–5)?
- What were the principal themes of Paul's preaching in Ephesus?
- What place did "power encounters" with occult forces play in the ministry in Philippi and Ephesus?
- Why was it that Paul's ministry brought him into conflict with civil authorities in at least four cities?
- Why was Paul so eager to get to Rome (see Romans 1:8–15), and what did he do when he got there (Acts 28:11ff)?
- What were the main characteristics of Paul's mission to these different cities?
- How do they prepare us in ministering to *outsiders* today?

STUDY 11

# Reaching the Outsider Today

- Who are the outsiders in your community?
- How good is your church at welcoming and ministering to the outsider?
- What further provision could be made?
- What do you think are the main lessons you have learnt from these studies in Luke and reading this book?
- How have your attitudes changed?
- If you were to do one thing as a result of these studies, what would it be?

# Notes

1. Alfred Plummer, *A Critical and Exegetical Commentary on the Gospel According to St. Luke ICC* (T. and T. Clark, 1975), pp. xx-xxii; John Drane, *Introducing the New Testament* (Lion Books, 1999), p. 200.

2. Robin Griffin–Jones, *The Four Witnesses: The Rebel, the Rabbi, the Chronicler, and the Mystic* (HarperOne, 2000).

3. Quoted in Eusebius, *History of the Church*, tr. G. A. Williamson (Penguin, 1989), 4.14.7.

4. Plummer, op. cit., pp. xxiii-xxix; Drane, op. ct., pp. 182–3.

5. Drane, op. cit., pp. 167–95.

6. F. F. Bruce, "The Synoptic Gospels", *New Bible Dictionary* (Inter Varsity Press, 1982).

7. Drane, op. cit., p. 216; I. Howard Marshall, *Luke: Historian and Theologian* (Inter Varsity Press, 1998), p.13.

8. Hans Conzelmann, *Die Mitte der Zeit* (J. C. B. Mohr, 1954); Hans Conzelmann, *An Outline of the Theology of the New Testament*, tr. J. Bowden (Harper & Row, 1969); Rudolph Bultmann, The *History of the Synoptic Tradition*, tr. John Marsh (Hendrickson, 1994); Günther Bornkamm, *The New Testament: A Guide to Its Writings* (Fortress Press, 1973).

9. Plummer, op. cit., p. xli.

10. Joseph Ratzinger, *Jesus of Nazareth: The Infancy Narratives* (Bloomsbury Publishing, 2012), p. 92–93.

11. Marshall, op. cit., p. 52.

12. Ibid., p. 54.

13. Ibid., p. 64.

14. Ratzinger, op. cit., p. 33.

15. Her family connection to Elizabeth may have made her a Levite too, but we cannot be sure.

16. Tom Holland, *Rubicon: The Triumph and Tragedy of the Roman Republic* (Abacus, 2003), p. 387.

17. Robin Lane Fox, *The Classical World: An Epic History of Greece and Rome* (Penguin, 2005), p. 506.

18. Kenneth E. Bailey, *Jesus through Middle Eastern Eyes: Cultural Studies in the Gospels* (SPCK 2008).

19. Marshall, op. cit., p. 158.

20. Ibid., p. 159.

21. Ibid., p. 161.

22. Bailey, op. cit., p. 152.

23. Ibid., p. 152.

24. Marshall, op. cit., p. 18.

25. Bailey op. cit., pp. 153–155.

26. Ibid., p. 151.

27. Ibid., pp. 149 ff.

28. Marshall, op. cit., p. 292.

29. Ibid., p. 280.

30. Some, like T. Zahn, argue that she was an adulteress; see T. Zahn, *Das Evangelium des Lucas* (Leipzig: 1913), p. 322, and Marshall, op. cit., p. 308.

31. Marshall, op. cit., p. 308.

32. Wolf, Miroslav, *Free of Charge: Giving and Forgiving in a Culture Stripped of Grace* (Zonderven, 2005), p. 121.

33. Bailey, op. cit., p. 173.

34. Ibid., p. 173.

35. Plummer, op. cit., p. xli.

36. Ibid., p. xli.

37. Joachim Jeremias, *Jerusalem in the Time of Jesus* (SCM Press, 1969), pp. 233ff.

38. Joachim Jeremias, *The Parables of Jesus* (Scribner, 1972), p. 203.

39. Ibid., p. 204.

40. Ibid., p. 128; Deuteronomy 21:17.

41. Jeremias, op. cit., p. 129.

42. J. M. Henri Nouwen, *The Return of the Prodigal Son: A Story of Homecoming* (Darton, Longman and Todd, 1998), pp. 40–41.

43. Ibid., p. 46.

44. Helmut Thielicke, *The Waiting Father: Sermons on the Parables of Jesus* (Harper & Row, 1959).

45. Nouwen, op. cit., p. 96.

46. Jeremias, op. cit., p. 141.

47. Ibid., op. cit., p. 309.

48. Ibid., p. 177.

49. Bailey, op. cit., p. 314.

50. Marshall, op. cit., p. 751.

51. Gregory of Nyssa, *From Glory to Glory*, tr. Jean Danielou (St Vladimir Seminary Press, 1997).

52. Ibid., p. 33.

53. Oliver James, *Affluenza* (Vermilion, 2007)

54. Ibid., p. 21.

55. Marshall, op. cit., p. 633.

56. Bailey, op. cit., p. 382.

57. Marshall, op. cit., p. 635.

58. James, op. cit., pp. 4–23.

59. St Basil the Great, *On Social Justice*, tr. C. Paul Schroeder (St Vladimir's Seminary Press, 2009), p. 59.

60. Ibid., p. 62.

61. Ibid., p. 66.

62. Joachim Jeremias, *The Parables of Jesus* (SCM Press, 2003), p. 58ff.

63. Marshall, op. cit., p. 704.

64. Ibid., p. 709.

65. Ibid., p. 619.

66. Ibid., p. 619.

67. Bailey, op. cit., p. 176.

68. Tom Wright, *How God became King: Getting to the heart of the Gospels* (London: SPCK, 2012).

69. Ibid., p. 158 and p. 240.

70. Quoted in ibid., p. 157.

71. "Euangelisasthai me dei"; literally "it behoves me to preach".

72. See Patrick Whitworth, *Becoming a Citizen of God's Kingdom* (TerraNova Publications, 2006).

73. George Eldon Ladd, *The Gospel of the Kingdom* (Paternoster Press, 1981).

74. Graham Tomlin, *The Prodigal Spirit: The Trinity, the Church and the Future of the World* (MPG Books, 2011), p. 53.

75. Ibid., pp. 52–3.

76. St Basil the Great, *On the Holy Spirit*, tr. Stephen Hildebrand, ed. John Behr (St Vladimir's Seminary Press, 2011), p. 53.

77. Patrick Whitworth, *Conversations with Jesus* (ReSource, 2013), ch. 8.

78. Isaiah 51:3; Marshall, op. cit., p. 872.

79. David J. Bosch, *Transforming Mission: Paradigm Shifts in Theology of Mission* (Orbis Books, 2005), p.88.

80. Marshall, op. cit., p. 35.

81. Bosch, op. cit., p. 91.

82. Stott, op. cit., p. 281.

83. John R. W. Stott, *The Message of Acts* (IVP, 1990), p. 285.

84. Ibid.

85. St Augustine of Hippo, *Confessions*, tr. Henry Chadwick (Oxford University Press, 2008), p. 3.

86. Patrick Whitworth, *The Word from the Throne: Themes from St John's writings for today's Church* (Donghong Co. Ltd., 2011).

87. Eugene Peterson, *A Long Obedience in the Same Direction* (Inter Varsity Press, 2000).

88. *The Epistle of Mathetes to Diognetus*, tr. Alexander Roberts and James Donaldson in Roberts, Alexander *et al* (eds.), *Ante-Nicene Fathers* (Buffalo, NY: Christian Literature Publishing Co., 1885), vol. 1, ch. v.

89. Martin Buber, *Ich und Du (I and Thou)*, tr. Charles Scribner (London: Continuum, 2004). Buber's philosophy is based around the idea of "existence is encounter".

90. Gregory of Nyssa, *On the difference between Essence and Hypostasis*; and see *Basil Letters 1–58*, 38, tr. Roy Deferrari (Harvard University Press, 1926). Quoted in Bishop Kallistos Ware, *The Orthodox Way* (St Vladimir's Seminary Press, 1979).

# Bibliography

Bailey, Kenneth E., *Jesus Through Middle Eastern Eyes: Cultural Studies in the Gospels* (SPCK, 2008).

Basil the Great, *On Social Justice*, tr. C. Paul Schroeder (St Vladimir's Seminary Press, 2009).

St Basil the Great, *On the Holy Spirit*, tr. Stephen Hildebrand, ed. John Behr (St Vladimir's Seminary Press, 2011)

Bosch, David J., *Transforming Mission: Paradigm Shifts in Theology of Mission* (Orbis Books, 2005).

Bruce, F. F., "The Synoptic Gospels", *New Bible Dictionary* (Inter Varsity Press, 1982).

Bruce, F. F., *Paul, Apostle of the Free Spirit* (Paternoster Press, 1977).

Drane, John, *Introducing the New Testament* (Lion Books, 1999).

Eusebius, *History of the Church*, tr. G. A. Williamson (Penguin, 1989).

Gregory of Nyssa, *From Glory to Glory*, tr. Jean Danielou (St Vladimir Seminary Press, 1997).

Griffith-Jones, Robin, *The Four Witnesses: The Rebel, the Rabbi, the Chronicler, and the Mystic* (HarperOne, 2000).

Holland, Tom, *Rubicon: The Triumph and Tragedy of the Roman Republic* (Abacus, 2003).

Howard Marshall, I., *Luke: Historian and Theologian* (Inter Varsity Press, 1998).

Howard Marshall, I., *The Gospel of Luke* (Paternoster Press, 1978).

Jeremias, Joachim, *Jerusalem in the Time of Jesus* (SCM Press, 1969).

Jeremias, Joachim, *The Parables of Jesus* (SCM Press, 2003).

Ladd, George Eldon, *The Gospel of the Kingdom* (Paternoster Press, 1981).

Lane Fox, Robin, *The Classical World: An Epic History of Greece and Rome* (Penguin, 2005).

Lewis, C. S., *The Four Loves* (HarperCollins, 2002).

Nouwen, Henri J. M., *The Return of the Prodigal Son: A Story of Homecoming* (Darton, Longman and Todd, 1998).

Oliver, James, *Affluenza* (Vermilion, 2007).

Plummer, Alfred, *A Critical and Exegetical Commentary on the Gospel According to St. Luke ICC* (T. and T. Clark, 1975).

Ratzinger, Joseph, *Jesus of Nazareth: The Infancy Narratives* (Bloomsbury Publishing, 2012).

Stott, John R. W., *The Message of Acts* (IVP, 1990). ✓

Sudworth, Richard, *Distinctly Welcoming* (Scripture Union, 2007).

Tomlin, Graham, *The Prodigal Spirit: The Trinity, the Church and the Future of the World* (MPG Books, 2011).

Whitworth, Patrick, *Conversations with Jesus* (ReSource, 2013).

Whitworth, Patrick, *Becoming a Citizen of the Kingdom* (TerraNova Publications, 2006).

Whitworth, Patrick, *The Word from the Throne: Themes from St John's writings for today's Church* (Donghong Co. Ltd., 2011)

Wolf, Miroslav, *Free of Charge: Giving and Forgiving in a Culture Stripped of Grace* (Zondervan, 2005).

Wright, Tom, *How God became King: Getting to the heart of the Gospels* (SPCK, 2012).

Wright, Tom, *Luke for Everyone* (SPCK, 2001).